SOCRATES, SPORT, AND STUDENTS

A Philosophical Inquiry into
Physical Education and Sport

Sheryle Bergmann Drewe

University Press of America,® Inc.
Lanham · New York · Oxford

Copyright © 2001 by
University Press of America,® Inc.
4720 Boston Way
Lanham, Maryland 20706

12 Hid's Copse Rd.
Cumnor Hill, Oxford OX2 9JJ

Library of Congress Cataloging-in-Publication Data

Drewe, Sheryle Bergmann.
Socrates, sport, and students : a philosophical inquiry into
physical education and sport / Sheryle Bergmann Drewe.
p. cm
Includes bibliographical references and index.
1. Physical education and training—Philosophy. 2. Sports—
Philosophy. 3. Physical education and training—Study and
teaching. 4. Sports—Study and teaching. I. Title.

GV342 .D74 2001   613.7'01—dc21   2001041484 CIP

ISBN 0-7618-2080-9 (cloth : alk. paper)

For Nick
With whom I share so much love
for philosophy, for life,
for each other

Contents

Preface

Socrates, Sport, and Students arose out of a need to counter attempts to eliminate or limit the time dedicated to physical education in schools. In this time of increased technology, cost-cutting and the back-to-basics movement, the value of physical education has been questioned in many curricular content debates. If physical education is to retain a place in the educational curriculum, a strong argument must be proposed. This book, in providing such an argument, should appeal to physical educators and administrators interested in justifying their activity. The book will also appeal to philosophers and professors in the areas of education, particularly physical education, and sport.

Socrates, Sport, and Students is unique in that it involves a philosophical approach to the concepts and issues involved in the practical world of physical education and sport. Although applied philosophers have recently been turning their attention towards sport, minimal work has been conducted concerning philosophy of physical education. There is an intimate connection between physical education and sport and to fully understand sport in our society, it is important to understand children's and youth's experiences in physical education. Physical education can play an important role in the educative experience of children and youth and this experience has the potential to transcend the schooling context into the world of sport–a world that is very pervasive in our society.

Acknowledgments

I would like to acknowledge the assistance provided by the Social Sciences and Humanities Research Council of Canada, the University of Manitoba, and the Health, Leisure and Human Performance Institute at the University of Manitoba, who provided grant money that facilitated the conducting of this research.

I would like to thank the many colleagues who generously suggested resources, and provided feedback on my work, particularly, John Colbeck, Dan Bailis, and Murray Elliot. I also want to thank the athletes and coaches who shared with me their thoughts concerning ethical issues and sport.

I must also acknowledge the publishers who kindly granted permission to republish articles, in part or in whole, which originally appeared in the following journals: Canadian Philosophy of Education Society's Bergmann Drewe, S. "Acquiring Practical Knowledge: A Justification for Physical Education," *Paideusis*, 12: 33-44, 1999; Kluwer Academic Publishers' Bergmann Drewe, S. "The Value of Knowledge/Rationality or the Knowledge/Rationality of Values: Implications for Education," *Studies in Philosophy and Education*, 20: 233-242, 2000; SAGE's Bergmann Drewe, S. "Competing Conceptions of Competition: Implications for Physical Education," *European Physical Education Review*, 4: 5-20, 1998; National Association for Physical Education in Higher Education [published by Human Kinetics]'s Bergmann Drewe, S. "An Examination of the Relationship Between Coaching and Teaching," *Quest*, 52: 79-88, 2000; Canadian Association for Health, Physical Education, Recreation and Dance's Bergmann Drewe, S. & Daniel, M. F. "The Fundamental Role of Critical Thinking in Physical Education," *Avante*, 4: 20-38, 1998 and

Bergmann Drewe, S. "Aesthetics and Sport: Commonalities and Contrasts," *Avante*, 5: 1-17, 1999; Taylor and Francis Ltd. [Rankine Road, Basington, Hants, RG24 8PR, UK]'s Bergmann Drewe, S. "The Logical Connection Between Moral Education and Physical Education," *Journal of Curriculum Studies*, 32: 561-574, 2000, Bergmann Drewe, S. "Moral Reasoning in Sport: Implications for Physical Education," *Sport, Education and Society*, 4: 117-130, 1999, and Bergmann Drewe, S. "Coaches, Ethics and Autonomy," *Sport, Education and Society*, 5: 147-162, 2000.

I must also thank my family and friends, who have been a constant source of support–both in encouraging my work and reiterating the need for a balanced life!

Finally, a special thanks to two very important guys in my life–to my son Josh who puts up with my writing while watching videos, and to my husband Nick who does not! Thanks for always being there.

Introduction

The start of this new millennium brings with it an incredible increase in technology and an accompanying demand for the creation and transmission of knowledge. This situation places an enormous burden on schools to determine how they can best prepare students to enter this technological age. With a finite number of hours in the school day, school administrators have to determine which of the multitude of available activities should be the focus for their students. These time constraints are accompanied by financial concerns. There is only so much money to hire teachers, offer various programs, and purchase equipment and supplies. Finally, along with dealing with time and monetary concerns, school boards have to deal with a constant demand to make sure all students are literate and numerate by the time they leave school. The demand for a back-to-basics education seems to fly in the face of a booming technological age, but the reality is that some students are completing their schooling without having acquired basic literacy and numeracy skills.

All of these demands have required those concerned with education, for example, ministers of education, school boards, school administrators, to debate various curricular options and many worthy activities have come "under the knife." One program that faces the criticism that it is not "technological" or "basic" and that specialist teachers are too costly, is physical education. The criticism faced by physical education exists worldwide as witnessed by the international call for physical education which came out of the Third International Conference of Ministers and Senior Officials Responsible for Physical Education and Sport (MINEPS III) held in Punta del Este, Uruguay in 1999. One of the documents endorsed by the conference, the *Berlin Agenda for Action,* called for *all* governments to increase their commitment to physical education for young people. In keeping with this call, I will also examine the advocacy literature put out by the

Canadian Association for Health, Physical Education, Recreation and Dance, as well as the American Alliance for Health, Physical Education, Recreation and Dance. In examining the advocacy documents, I will propose that an important argument is missing in these documents and *Socrates, Sport, and Students* is an attempt to rectify this situation.

MINEPS III endorsed three documents: *The Berlin Agenda for Action*, *The Declaration of Punta del Este*, and the *MINEPS III Recommendations*. *The Berlin Agenda for Action* gives reasons for taking steps to reinforce the importance of physical education. The Agenda proposes that physical education: is the most effective and inclusive means of providing all children with skills, attitudes, values, knowledge, and understanding for life-long participation in physical activity and sport; helps to ensure integrated and rounded development of mind, body, and spirit; is the only school subject whose primary focus is on the body, physical activity, physical development, and health; helps children develop the patterns of and interest in physical activity, which are essential for healthy development, and which lay the foundations for adult healthy lifestyles; helps children develop respect for their own and other's bodies; develops understanding of the roles of physical activity in promoting health; contributes to children's self-confidence and self-esteem; enhances social development by preparing children to cope with competition, winning and losing, and co-operation and collaboration; and provides skills and knowledge for future work in sport, physical activity, recreation, and leisure, growing areas of employment.

The Declaration of Punta del Este also proposes a few reasons for why governments should reinforce the importance of physical education. The Declaration states that physical education and sport is an essential element and an integral part of education and human and social development, as well as a contributing factor for social cohesion, mutual tolerance and the integration of different ethnic and cultural minorities. This Declaration also suggests that physical education plays a role in reducing juvenile delinquency and violence, and rising medical and social costs.

It is interesting to note how many of the reasons given in the Agenda and Declaration for reinforcing the importance of physical education have to do with promoting health, both physical and mental, for example, respect for bodies, self-confidence, self-esteem and social development and cohesion. This emphasis on health is also prominent in the advocacy materials put out by the Canadian Association for Health, Physical Education, Recreation and Dance (CAHPERD), as well as the American Alliance for Health, Physical Education, Recreation and Dance (AAHPERD). CAHPERD has published two resources for advocacy purposes: *Making the Case for Physical Education in Canada* and *Destination QDPE [Quality Daily Physical Education]: An Information Kit*. *Making the Case for Physical Education in Canada* does not provide reasons why physical education is beneficial other than the benefits they cite for physical *activity*, that is, improved psychological well-being, improved health and quality of life, improved behaviour and ability to learn, better health habits, and reduction of health care costs. *Destination QDPE* does make reference to benefits resulting from a Quality Daily Physical Education program. The brochures provided in this kit suggest that children participating in Quality Daily Physical Education programs: come to class ready to learn and demonstrate improved concentration, enhanced creativity and better task performance and problem solving skills; play better with others; display improved individual and class behavior; have excellent aerobic endurance, muscular strength and fewer risk factors for cardiovascular and other diseases; experience optimal growth and development; experience improved self-esteem and self-concept, and lower levels of anxiety and stress; perform as well, or better, academically compared to those receiving more academic curriculum time and less physical education; develop positive attitudes about school, physical activity and themselves, leading to improved attendance and a reduction in school drop out rates; have better health habits and are less likely to smoke and engage in the use of drugs and alcohol; develop lifelong, personal physical activity habits; and enjoy physical education classes.

AAHPERD has recently published a *Sport and Physical Education Advocacy Kit II*. This kit contains a section entitled "Why Children Need Physical Education?" where the following benefits are attributed to participation in physical education programs: improved physical fitness; support of other subject areas; self-discipline [regarding health and fitness]; skill development; experience setting goals; regular, healthful physical activity; improved judgment [in the moral domain]; improved self-confidence and self-esteem; stress reduction; and strengthened peer relationships. Once again, the reasons cited for participating in physical education lean heavily on physical and mental health topics, for example, fitness, self-confidence, self-esteem, stress reduction, peer relationships.

In critiquing the advocacy material put out by the World Summit on Physical Education, CAHPERD, and AAHPERD, I am not denying the benefits these organizations attribute to physical education programs. However, the most prominent benefits espoused have to do with improving physical and mental health, for example, improving respect for bodies, self-confidence, self-esteem, social development and cohesion, fitness, stress reduction, growth and development, and personal physical activity habits. The problem is that these physical and mental health objectives could be met through other programs, both curricular and extracurricular. For example, improved self-confidence and self-esteem could result from exposure to an arts curriculum, where students are encouraged to express themselves through various media. Physical fitness, discipline, and stress reduction could be achieved by participating in recreation programs such as soccer clubs, or initiating one's own running program. The problem with most of the reasons cited by the leading organizations promoting physical education is that the reasons are instrumental; that is, the same benefits could be achieved through different means. Thus, these justificatory arguments are not unique to physical education. A more detailed discussion of instrumental arguments will occur in chapter one.

What is required for providing a strong argument for the inclusion of physical education in the curriculum is an argument that is intrinsic to the act of educating. The closest any of the advocacy material comes to acknowledging the role of physical education as *educating* students are some posters in *Making the Case for Physical Education in Canada*. These posters have pictures of sporting equipment wearing graduation caps with the slogan "Help your child to learn!" across the top. However, the material does not detail *how* physical education helps children to learn. In fact, the only references to learning in the *Destination QDPE* is that children involved in Quality Daily Physical Education programs come to class ready to learn and demonstrate improved concentration, enhanced creativity and better task performance and problem solving skills; and perform as well, or better, academically compared to those receiving more academic curriculum time and less physical education. What these references are referring to is the role of physical education in improving learning in the classroom, not necessarily in the gymnasium.

Education is intimately tied to the acquisition of knowledge and what the advocates of physical education have not been stressing is that physical education is *education* in the sense that students are acquiring knowledge, in this case, practical knowledge. Although physical education is not unique in providing opportunities to acquire practical knowledge (e.g., students conducting science experiments rely on the acquisition of practical knowledge), as I will argue in chapter five, physical education is unique in requiring a logical connection between acquiring practical knowledge and practicing moral education. Stressing the practical and moral knowledge required in physical education programs provides a stronger argument than relying on the instrumental arguments concerning health and fitness so often espoused by advocates of physical education.

Socrates, Sport, and Students proposes a strong argument for the inclusion of physical education in the school system. This justification relies on arguing for the possibility of acquiring practical knowledge through physical education programs. Practical knowledge would be entailed in "knowing how" as opposed to "knowing that" and the development of this form of knowledge should be a fundamental aim of physical education.

Arguing for the importance of practical knowledge (chapter one) and the role physical education plays in helping students acquire this knowledge (chapter two) ushers in the topics of critical thinking (chapter three), competition (chapter four), moral education (chapter five), the relationship between coaches and athletes (chapters six and seven), and the relationship between physical education and sport (chapters eight and nine).

If practical knowledge involves "learning how" to do something, then physical educators should help students achieve excellence in whatever activity the students are learning how to do. Striving for excellence requires an element of competition. The origin of the word *com-petitio* is to "strive together." Students need to "strive together" to compare themselves with someone or a standard set by someone in order to determine whether they have achieved their potential.

The competitive situation that I am advocating is one that involves a respect for mutually agreed upon rules as well as a respect for opponents as persons. This respect for rules and opponents is not always evident in competitive situations and if we are to achieve *competitio*, a significant component of the physical education program must be concerned with moral education. Moral education can take a number of forms and teaching by example and by precept are both necessary for students to acquire the moral reasoning required for *competitio* to be realized.

An important aspect of both the acquisition of practical knowledge and the moral education required to participate in competitive situations that facilitate the development of practical knowledge is the fostering of critical thinking. Critical thinking is required in "knowing how" to perform a physical skill, for example, analyzing what has gone wrong when a golf swing does not result in a good shot; or in playing a game, for example, judging where a volleyball should be aimed in order that the opposing team cannot return it; and so forth. Critical thinking is also required in developing moral reasons for respecting rules and opponents. For example, participants in a competitive activity must understand moral principles such as fairness and respect for others and then apply these principles to specific situations.

Whether athletes do apply moral principles to specific situations is more of an empirical rather than philosophical question. Thus, I interviewed university level athletes to ascertain the kind of ethical issues they faced and how they resolved them. The athletes commented on how their moral reasoning was influenced by their coach. I then interviewed university level coaches to determine the ethical issues they faced as well as how much autonomy they thought their athletes should have when it came to making ethical decisions.

The issue of autonomy and athletes raises the question of the relationship between coaching and teaching. An important aim of education is to develop autonomous individuals. Coaches should view themselves more as teachers and encourage the development of autonomy in their athletes, as well as expand their view of the coach's job beyond the "narrow" development of physical skill acquisition.

Although I propose narrowing the gap between coaching and teaching, I do recognize the different functions played by sport and physical education in our society. I admit that not all sport is education, for example, recreational and professional, and that physical education is not simply sport. Human movement involves both functional and expressive aspects and sport involves mainly functional movements. Thus, I conclude with an examination of the relationship between physical education, sport, and aesthetic experience.

In this time of increased technology, cost-cutting and the back-to-basics movement, physical education has been "under the knife" in many curricular content debates. If physical education is to retain a place in the educational curriculum, a strong argument must be proposed. The purpose of this book is to provide such an argument.

Chapter 1

A Justification for Physical Education Based on the Acquisition of Practical Knowledge

During this time of cost-cutting and the back-to-the-basics movement, physical educators must provide persuasive arguments for the inclusion of physical education in the school curriculum. Physical education is typically justified as a means for students to achieve healthy and fit lifestyles. However, this instrumental justification is a weak form of argument, for there are other means of becoming healthy and fit. For example, someone who walks or runs on a regular basis can achieve a reasonable fitness level and walking and running are basic motor skills which most people are able to achieve outside of a school curriculum. Thus, a more persuasive argument for the inclusion of physical education in an *educational* curriculum is required. I will argue that a justification intrinsic to the notion of education that justifies physical education based on the development of practical knowledge provides a strong argument for the inclusion of physical education in the educational curriculum.

Instrumental Justification

Physical education is frequently advocated as a valuable means to helping students achieve fit and healthy lifestyles. I am not disputing this claim. The importance of fitness cannot be over-estimated. In Scott Kretchmar's words:

Physical fitness . . . affects all of us, athlete and non-athlete alike, by
modifying what we can do, how long we can do it, how we feel, and how
well we regard ourselves. . . . Fitness is also the closest thing we have to a
necessary means value. In that fitness promotes continued life itself, it is
absolutely necessary to all end values.[1]

Although the value of fit and healthy lifestyles is not being disputed,
justifying the inclusion of physical education in an *educational*
curriculum based upon this claim is problematic. Justifying the
inclusion of physical education based upon its potential for achieving
health and fitness utilizes an instrumental argument. Jim Parry makes
three objections regarding an instrumental argument. First, it is a weak
form of argument because of its hypothetical and contingent nature.
"This is tantamount to saying, for example, that sport is of value *only if*
it contributes to health, and it becomes a matter of contingent fact
whether or not sports actually *does* contribute to health."[2] Thus, the
uncertainty and temporary justification of an instrumental argument
must be considered in our endeavor to justify physical education as a
curriculum component.

A second objection to the instrumental argument concerns the move
made from a moral argument to a factual one. "We begin by enquiring
into the value of PE [physical education] activities, but we now find
ourselves asking the quite different question of whether or not (and to
what extent) a particular activity *as a matter of fact* serves some other
value."[3] This move avoids the moral question by presupposing the
value of health or fitness and viewing physical education as valuable
only in instrumental terms. The third objection is that the instrumental
argument turns the argument concerning physical education into an
argument about something else, for example health or fitness. "The
Health-Related Fitness movement accepts the value of a certain
definition of fitness and health, and judges all PE [physical education]
activities against this fitness/health value. No wonder that PE [physical
education] activities become marginalized."[4] The example mentioned
previously of encouraging students to walk or run on a regular basis
could fulfill the fitness/health value and thus there would be no need
for participation in other physical education activities.

I must emphasize at this point that I am not denying that there are
instrumental values to participation in physical education. I am only
suggesting that an instrumental argument, for the reasons cited above,
is not strong enough to provide a persuasive justification for the
inclusion of physical education in the curriculum. To quote Parry once

again, "Instrumental justifications, though sometimes useful if sensibly deployed, must be seen as at best ancillary benefits to a subject which stands or falls by the strength of its primary rationale, which will be intrinsic and educational."[5]

A Justification Intrinsic to the Notion of Education

In 1979, David Carr wrote an article entitled "Aims of Physical Education" in which he provided an intrinsic justification for the inclusion of physical education as an educational activity. At the present time, when physical education is fighting for its survival in the face of cost-cutting and the back-to-the-basics movement, it would seem of utmost importance that we revisit this argument.[6] In naming this section "A Justification Intrinsic to the Notion of Education," my affinity for the R. S. Peters and Paul Hirst notion of a liberal education becomes evident. In the light of much postmodern writing, the notion of a liberal education having anything to do with "knowledge" might seem a little passe. However, I want to revive Peters's argument and then expand his conception of knowledge to include practical, as well as theoretical knowledge.

Peters examines processes of education and suggests that "to educate someone implies not only some sort of achievement, but also one that is worthwhile. It also implies that the manner of doing this should not be morally objectionable."[7] In determining what sort of achievement is worthwhile, Peters points out that the answer lies in the question–that is, to ask the question presupposes a commitment to rationality. Thus, the sort of achievement that is worthwhile is the development of rationality. "Anyone who asks seriously the question 'Why do this rather than that?' must already possess it [rationality]; for it is built into this sense of 'serious.' It is impossible to give any further justification for it [rationality]; for it is presupposed in all serious attempts of justification."[8] The answer to the question concerning aims *of* education is singular–the development of rationality. The aims *in* education would involve tasks designed to develop rationality. Central to the development of rationality is the ability to think critically. Harvey Siegel illuminates the connection between rationality and critical thinking:

> To be a critical thinker is to be appropriately moved by reasons. To be a
> rational person is to believe and act on the basis of reasons. There is then

a deep conceptual connection, by way of the notion of reasons, between critical thinkers and rational persons. Critical thinking is best conceived, consequently, as the *educational cognate* of rationality.[9]

The importance of critical thinking for the development of rationality has been recognized in current educational practice. However, what has happened to some degree is that critical thinking has been perceived as an abstract skill, autonomous of disciplinary content. Peters points out the absurdness of this situation: "[I]t is equally absurd to foster an abstract skill called 'critical thinking' without handing on anything concrete to be critical about."[10] Thus, an important task designed to develop rationality would entail the "handing on" of something concrete. Peters describes this "handing on" as an initiation into inherited traditions:

> With the mastery of basic skills the door is opened to a vaster and more variegated inheritance. Further differentiation develops as the [student] becomes initiated more deeply into distinctive forms of knowledge such as science, history, mathematics, religious and aesthetic appreciation, and into the practical types of knowledge involved in moral, prudential, and technical forms of thought and action. . . . To have a mind . . . is to have an awareness differentiated in accordance with the canons implicit in all of these inherited traditions. "Education" marks out the processes by means of which the individual is initiated into them.[11]

Thus, according to Peters, aims *in* education involve helping students acquire the knowledge and understanding that are part of humankind's inherited traditions. These forms of knowledge are *intrinsic* to the educational task of developing a rational mind. It is the intrinsic value of the knowledge and understanding developed through educational processes wherein lies a persuasive justification for physical education activities.

However, before pursuing the connection between the aim of education and aims in physical education, we must address a postmodern criticism of Peters's account of education. Hirst and Peters suggest that the answer to the "what is the aim of education" question is either a conceptual truth or a persuasive definition. I (following Carr) have illuminated Hirst and Peters's account that suggests that the question of the aim of education is a conceptual truth having to do with the development of rationality through knowledge and understanding. However, the criticism could be raised that this is simply a persuasive definition of education. Carr phrases the criticism as follows: "We have, it will be said, just *preferred* to define education as the development of knowledge and understanding; but people at other times and in other places have been inclined to define it differently."[12] Although there *are* disagreements about the nature of education, Carr points out that these disagreements are not so much about the notion that education involves the development of knowledge and understanding but rather "about *what sorts* of knowledge and understanding are worth passing on to children or about *how* knowledge considered valuable should be inculcated."[13] It is to the question of what sorts of knowledge and understanding are worth passing on to students that we now turn.

Practical Knowledge

In the description cited by Peters on education as initiation into inherited traditions, he alludes to "the practical types of knowledge involved in moral, prudential, and technical forms of thought and action."[14] However, he does not elaborate on "practical types of knowledge" and his subsequent lack of reference to "technical forms of thought and action" has given the impression that he is only concerned with theoretical forms of knowledge. Hirst, likewise, has been criticized for concentrating almost exclusively upon theoretical knowledge in the educational curriculum. In Hirst's words:

> There is a central place in education for the arts and the practical, and that goes for all pupils. But the *educational significance of these is limited*, and any retreat from the demands of the many forms of language that are so central to human development is to set barriers to that development for many children (italics added). [15]

In fairness to Hirst, however, it must be noted that in a recent publication, he retracts his overemphasis on the theoretical. "Of course I now consider practical knowledge to be more fundamental than theoretical knowledge, the former being basic to any clear grasp of the proper significance of the latter."[16] The question that must be addressed at this point concerns the meaning and significance of "practical knowledge."

Aristotle spoke of "practical wisdom" which he distinguished from "scientific knowledge" as well as "art":

Therefore, since scientific knowledge involves demonstration, but there is no demonstration of things whose first principles are variable (for all such things might actually be otherwise), and since it is impossible to deliberate about things that are of necessity, practical wisdom cannot be scientific knowledge nor art; not science because that which can be done is capable of being otherwise, not art because action and making are different kinds of things. . . . The remaining alternative, then, is that it is a true and reasoned state of capacity to act with regard to the things that are good or bad for man.[17]

It is significant to note that Aristotle refers to "practical wisdom" as a "reasoned state." From this "practical reasoning," G. E. M. Anscombe derives the notion of "practical knowledge":

A man has practical knowledge who knows how to do things; but that is an insufficient description, for he *might* be said to know how to do things if he could give a lecture on it, though he was helpless when confronted with the task of doing them. When we ordinarily speak of practical knowledge we have in mind a certain sort of general capacity in a particular field; but if we hear of a capacity, it is reasonable to ask what constitutes an exercise of it.[18]

Anscombe makes an important point when she states that knowing how to do things is an insufficient description for practical knowledge. Confusion has arisen over this issue and this is due in part to a distinction made famous by Gilbert Ryle–a distinction between "knowing that" and "knowing how":

We speak of *learning how* to play an instrument as well as of *learning that* something is the case; of finding out *how to* prune trees as well as of *finding out that* the Romans had a camp in a certain place; of *forgetting how* to tie a reef-knot as well as of *forgetting that* the German for "knife" is "Messer" (italics added).[19]

Ryle elaborates on what it means to "know how" by suggesting that knowing how involves not only performing an operation correctly or successfully, but also applying criteria in performing critically. However, Ryle is quick to point out that when such a performance is referred to as an action exhibiting intelligence, one must be careful not to reassimilate "knowing how" to "knowing that":

"Intelligent" cannot be defined in terms of "intellectual" or "know *how*" in terms of "knowing *that*"; "thinking what I am doing" does not connote "both thinking what to do and doing it". When I do something intelligently, i.e., thinking what I am doing, I am doing one thing and not two. My performance has a special procedure or manner, not special antecedents.[20]

Ryle notes the infinite regress involved if it were the case that one had to consider a regulative proposition before executing a performance, since one would have to consider what makes one regulative proposition more appropriate than another and this would involve the consideration of another regulative proposition, and so forth. Rather, Ryle proposes that it is not the parentage but the procedure that makes a performance intelligent. It is Ryle's emphasis on the overt procedure as the criterion for assessing one's ability to "know how" that has elicited criticism and we turn now to Carr's examination of Ryle's behaviourist approach to "knowing how."

Carr makes an important point when he notes that "we can and do meaningfully attribute 'knowing how' to people who cannot themselves do the particular things in question. It seems . . . that the teaching of practical knowledge depends on this possibility."[21] Carr gives the examples of a near-retirement aged physical education teacher who continues to teach his students things that he is no longer able to do or the teachers who find themselves instructing students who possess far greater ability than they have in activities which they themselves are only able to perform poorly, if at all. These examples demonstrate that being able to do the activity in question is not a necessary condition for "knowing how" to do these activities. Being able to do the activity is also not a sufficient condition for one to be described as "knowing how" to do an activity. Carr gives the example of someone picking up darts for the first time and scoring a bullseye on the first throw. This "beginner's luck" situation raises the question of intentionality as a critical component of practical knowledge.

In analyzing what we mean by intention, Stuart Hampshire proposes that:

What I do, in the sense of try to do, I necessarily know that I do, in that use of "know". . . in which "knowing" does not necessarily imply "being able to state correctly". Others do not necessarily know what I am trying to do. . . . They have only seen or heard, or otherwise perceived or inferred, what I am trying to do. I have never perceived or inferred what I am trying to do; I have always and unavoidably known.[22]

"Knowing how" differs from "knowing that" in that one cannot necessarily "state correctly" what one knows in the "knowing how" situation. There are two concepts to be examined here–the ability to "state" and the ability to "state *correctly*." The "knowing how" situation does not always lend itself to easily stating what is happening in verbal terms. However, this is not to imply that "knowing how" is devoid of conceptual content. As Hampshire points out, "[W]hile we are awake and fully conscious, we are all the time acting and moving with intent, and for much of the time our thinking is practical thinking, issuing directly in intended action and not formulated in words."[23] Saul Ross elaborates on the employment of concepts in practical thinking:

> An agent executing an intentional action is conscious of what he is doing, and although he may not be able to express the concepts verbally, he employs them in the judgments he renders and the decisions he makes. The thoughts that guide and direct his actions are conceptual in nature even if they cannot be stated propositionally; these practical concepts are manifested in intentional actions.[24]

Ross gives an illuminating example to demonstrate how judgements made during an intentional action are not always brought to consciousness. He points out that when we walk under normal circumstances, we are not consciously aware of the decisions we make regarding our action. However, if we attempt to walk on a slippery incline, all of our attention is directed to the placement of each step, "[E]ach decision is made explicitly and we are fully conscious of 'thinking out' each step along the way."[25] He suggests that "a similar situation applies in the process of actions as we move in our usual manner within familiar surroundings; judging, selecting and making decisions are inherent in action."[26]

Thus, although it is not always easy to verbalize what we know when we "know how," the preceding examples are illustrations that we can, upon reflection, "state" what we know how to do. The notion of "state *correctly*" raises another issue altogether–that of truth conditions. The traditional view of knowledge requires that to know *x*, one must have a justified, true belief that *x* is so. Is there a parallel to such conditions regarding practical knowledge? Hampshire would answer in the negative: "This scheme of deliberate action, and of the form of explanation appropriate to it, can scarcely be appraised as either true or false; for it is not clear what could be the basis of assessment, or what kind of evidence could be decisive."[27]

Carr takes up the challenge of providing a basis of assessment for practical knowledge situations. He proposes for the assessment of practical knowledge, conditions parallel to those utilized for theoretical knowledge, that is, the conditions of justified, true belief. He suggests that for one to know how to do x, one must 1) entertain $x$ing as a purpose, 2) be acquainted with a set of practical procedures for successful $x$ing, and 3) exhibit recognizable success at $x$ing.[28] Entertaining $x$ing as a purpose involves the notion of intentionality discussed earlier and Carr suggests that "[o]ur familiar understanding of exercises of knowing how is that they are the expressions of deliberate purposes . . . just as our ordinary understanding of knowing that acknowledges that what is known is also usually believed."[29] The condition of being acquainted with a set of practical procedures for successful $x$ing is analogous to providing a justification for a propositional knowledge claim. To substantiate this claim, Carr advocates Aristotle's notion of practical inference: "It is A's purpose to x; A understands that $y$ing is a satisfactory way to x; A ys."[30]

Such a form of inference offers us a way to demonstrate just how simple or basic actions from which complicated skills are built—relate to one another as means to ends. In general, then, there is no more reason to deny that relations of a logical kind may hold between the characterisations of the individual actions that are parts of the complicated patterns of activity that are exercises of knowing how, than there is to deny that such relations also hold between the descriptions of the judgements that offer logical or evidential support for a given bit of knowing that.[31]

Being acquainted with a set of practical procedures for successful $x$ing is one condition for "knowing how" but the final condition involves exhibiting recognizable success at $x$ing. This condition would be analogous to the truth condition of a propositional knowledge claim. Although Carr does admit that what one knows how to do is not a proposition but an action and thus can be neither true nor false, he adopts Anthony Kenny's argument that since practical reasoning is more closely related to imperative than to indicative reasoning, the concept of satisfactoriness rather than truth should be regarded as the validating principle.

Whereas in standard theoretical inference, the main concern is that from a set of true judgements a true conclusion should be validly inferred, what is sought through practical inferences are effective or satisfactory ways to adapt the world to often complex human purposes.[32]

Students should have the opportunity to acquire practical knowledge and this can only be accomplished through practical reasoning.

Learning to perform a given complex task or coming to know how to do it is essentially a matter of learning to reason practically and teaching someone how to execute a particular purpose is similarly a matter of instructing him in practical reasoning by means of practical directives; of acquainting him with rational procedures and showing him how particular ends are logically related to specific means.[33]

To not provide students an opportunity to engage in practical reasoning would leave a significant void in their education. Thus, a course such as physical education that involves a large degree of practical reasoning should be viewed as an important component of an educational curriculum.

Knowing About, In and Through the Physical

The preceding section involved an examination of the nature and significance of practical knowledge. Although the teaching and learning of practical knowledge is what distinguishes physical education from more primarily theoretical knowledge components of the educational curriculum, for example, mathematics or history, it would be remiss of me not to examine the other areas of knowledge which constitute physical education. Peter Arnold presents what he refers to as a "three dimensional model of the movement curriculum"[34] and this model provides a suitable framework for organizing the varieties of knowledge involved in physical education. Arnold gives these dimensions "catchy" titles but to avoid succumbing to a mind/body dualism, we must be mindful of their metaphorical nature. Arnold refers to the three dimensions of movement as: 1) education *about* movement, 2) education *in* movement, and 3) education *through* movement. Education *in* movement refers to the practical knowledge discussed in the previous section. I will now examine the knowledge involved in education *about* and *through* movement.

"Education *about* movement" would involve the teaching and learning of theoretical and factual knowledge pertaining to the discipline of physical education. A. D. Munrow divides this knowledge into three categories: 1) knowledge and understanding directly relevant to the specific skills or activities being taught, 2) knowledge and understanding of how the body works, and 3) knowledge in related fields. Knowledge and understanding directly relevant to the specific skills or activities being taught would include not only the knowledge and understanding of skill technique but also, as Harold Vanderzwaag points out, knowledge and understanding of the rules, etiquette, strategy, terminology and jargon, and the equipment and facilities necessary to partake in a given activity. The knowledge and understanding of how the body works would include:

> [K]nowledge of procedures in the prevention and care of injuries; knowledge of the effects of exercise on the body; knowledge of mechanical principles in the performance of skills; knowledge of relevant anatomic structure and function of body systems; knowledge about methods to develop fitness and the benefits of fitness.[35]

Regarding knowledge in related fields, Earle Zeigler and K. J. McCristal organized the academic content of physical education into six specific areas: i) exercise physiology, ii) biomechanics, iii) motor learning and sports psychology, iv) sociology of sport education, v) history, philosophy, and comparative physical education and sport, and vi) administrative theory. Whether this is an appropriate organizational scheme is not the issue here; my concern is with the content of physical education's body of knowledge. What is evident is the large body of theoretical knowledge that incorporates knowledge from related fields into the discipline of physical education.

Turning now to an examination of education *through* movement, it is important to recognize that when education occurs *through* movement as opposed to *in* movement, we are speaking of movement being used in an instrumental sense. That is, participation in movement activities is being undertaken to further purposes *other* than the acquisition of practical knowledge. As mentioned earlier in this chapter, physical education is frequently advocated as a valuable means to helping students achieve fit lifestyles. Using movement to achieve fitness is an example of education *through* movement. Other examples of the instrumental value of movement would include the use of movement to contribute to the development of: self-knowledge, self-esteem and personhood, social education, health education, environmental education, moral education, and aesthetic education. As Derek Meakin points out: "Central to being a person is that one has a body. It seems reasonable therefore to claim that PE [physical education] can contribute saliently to the development of personhood by assisting pupils to develop physically."[36] Regarding moral education through physical education, Meakin emphasizes the moral values built into many competitive game rules: "That this is so can be illustrated by concrete examples of rules designed to promote fair play, consideration for others and more generally respect for persons."[37] Environmental education can be enhanced through outdoor pursuits such as hiking, canoeing, camping, skiing, and so forth. Aesthetic education can be enhanced through the appreciation of what David Best refers to as aesthetic sports, such as gymnastics, diving, and figure skating. Thus, there are aspects of many physical education activities that have the potential to further other curricular purposes.

The "Education" in Physical Education

In the preceding section, I presented something of a misnomer when I referred to *education* through movement. When movement is used instrumentally to achieve purposes other than participating for the intrinsic value of the activity, it would be more appropriate to refer to such activities as meeting *schooling* as opposed to *educational* objectives. In fairness to Arnold, whose three-dimensional model I have adopted, I must point out that he *does* make this distinction. He categorizes objectives such as those involved in moral education or aesthetic education through movement as *educational objectives* while objectives involving the promotion of health and fitness or social interaction as *objectives of schooling* (desirable but not strictly educative). To clarify this distinction, it is helpful to delve into the philosophy of education literature.

Cornel Hamm makes an important distinction between two uses of the term "education": the "institutional" use and the "general enlightenment" use.[38] The institutional use refers to formal "educational" institutions–that is, schools. This use of the term is the one being expressed in statements such as "I have had sixteen years of education" or "I am going to quit my job and continue my education." The "general enlightenment" use of the term "education" refers to something that may or may not go on in schools. Hamm proceeds to detail the "general enlightenment" use of "education" by examining Peters's account of education (recall our discussion in the earlier section on a justification intrinsic to the notion of education). If one reserves the term "education" for the "general enlightenment" use and "schooling" for the "institutional" use, we can make sense of the distinction made between educational objectives being met through movement and schooling objectives being met through movement. What is important to keep in mind here, however, is that both sorts of objectives are still utilizing movement in an instrumental sense.

Although I am not denying the value of using movement to promote fit and healthy lifestyles, social interaction, and so forth, or to enhance moral or aesthetic education, this attempt to justify a position for physical education in the educational curriculum neglects a much stronger justification—the justification which establishes physical education as a unique component of the educational curriculum with its primary focus on the acquisition of practical knowledge. I have proposed that such a justification is intrinsic to the notion of education and that to justify physical education based on the acquisition of practical knowledge provides a strong argument for the inclusion of physical education in the educational curriculum.

Chapter 2

The Relationship Between the Acquisition of Knowledge and the Educational Aim of Developing Rationality

In chapter one, I argued for the inclusion of physical education in the educational curriculum based on the potential for students to acquire practical knowledge through participation in physical activity. I expressed my affinity for the Peters and Hirst notion of a liberal education and assumed the value of a liberal education in my argument for physical education based on the acquisition of knowledge, practical as well as theoretical. However, the notion and value of a liberal education has come under attack in this postmodern age. Thus, to truly provide an argument for physical education based on the acquisition of knowledge, requires a justification of an education having anything to do with "knowledge." To present such a justification is the purpose of the present chapter.

A notion made popular by Peters and Hirst in the 1960's was the idea of knowledge being intrinsic to the educational enterprise. Hirst later summarized his and Peters's conception of educational aims as follows: "The aims were first and foremost those of developing knowledge and understanding and the further pursuit of those as being both intrinsically worthwhile and vital to the ordering of developments in all other aspects of personal and social living."[1] Hirst has subsequently changed his position on this "rationalist" approach toward education. Although his concerns need to be addressed, I want to argue that the acquisition of knowledge, along with the development of rationality, is still an important, in fact, *the* primary justification for educational experiences.

A number of questions must be addressed before concluding that the acquisition of knowledge intrinsic to education should be a primary justification for educational experiences. First of all, what is "knowledge intrinsic to education"? Does this sort of knowledge take precedence over knowledge that might be considered instrumental in some sense? The possibility of differing justificatory status for knowledge raises the question of the value of knowledge in the first place. Does the acquisition of knowledge in an educational enterprise require no further justification, that is, is knowledge inarguably valuable, or is knowledge just one value among other values? In this postmodern age, it would seem imperative to address this question.

The first section of the chapter will entail an explication of the justificatory argument for educational experiences based upon the acquisition of knowledge. A distinction will be made between knowledge considered intrinsic as opposed to knowledge considered to be instrumental in some sense, as well as an examination of these different justificatory statuses. The second section of the chapter will explore the notion of knowledge being just one value among other values, including an examination of what these other values might entail. I will then examine the relationship between the acquisition of knowledge and the concept of rationality. Finally, I will argue that the acquisition of knowledge in conjunction with rational thought is a unique value that should take precedence over other values when justifying educational experiences. I will conclude the chapter by illuminating the implications of the preceding argument for the practice of education.

Knowledge as Intrinsic or Instrumental

As I argued in chapter one, physical education advocates should not rely on the justification that participation in physical education improves students' health and fitness levels because such a justification relies on an instrumental as opposed to an intrinsic argument. I was not denying that there are instrumental values to participation in physical education. However, I was suggesting that an instrumental argument, for the reasons cited in chapter one, is not strong enough to provide a persuasive justification for the inclusion of physical education in the curriculum. To quote Parry once again, "Instrumental justifications, though sometimes useful if sensibly deployed, must be seen as at best ancillary benefits to a subject which stands or falls by the strength of its primary rationale, which will be intrinsic and educational."[2] But is a rationale based on "intrinsic and educational" grounds possible? This question must be answered if the justification for educational activity based upon the acquisition of "knowledge intrinsic to education" is to have any weight.

John White, in his book *The Aims of Education Restated,* critiques four attempts at demonstrating the "intrinsicness" of the aims of education. First, he rejects the attempt by Hirst and Peters who argue that it is analytically true that education must have intrinsic aims since they have defined "education" as the "initiation into intrinsically worthwhile activities." White points out that "such a move would not get us very far, since we would still need to know whether we should adopt this definition of education or reject it–which is tantamount to wondering what we were wondering in the first place, that is, whether aims should be intrinsic or not."[3] The second attempt White critiques is again based on the work of Hirst and Peters–the so-called "transcendental" argument. This argument is summed up by Hirst in the following manner:

> To ask for the justification of any form of activity is significant only if one is in fact committed already to seeking rational knowledge. To ask for a justification of the pursuit of rational knowledge itself therefore presupposes some form of commitment to what one is seeking to justify. Justification is possible only if what is being justified is both intelligible under publicly rooted concepts and is assessable according to accepted criteria. It assumes a commitment to these two principles. But these very principles are in fact fundamental to the pursuit of knowledge in all its forms, be it, for instance, empirical knowledge or understanding in the arts. The forms of knowledge are in a sense simply the working out of these general principles in particular ways.[4]

White is critical of the transcendental argument for at least two reasons. First, he argues that "the sceptic is not 'committed to the pursuit of knowledge' in the sense that educationists have in mind, that is, to the pursuit of some or other *branch* of knowledge . . . the most he is committed to seeking is the specific piece of knowledge which answers his question."[5] The second objection White has concerning the transcendental argument is that it does not show why knowledge is valuable *for its own sake,* "[S]ince there is no guarantee that the questioner has not extrinsic reasons for asking his question."[6]

The third approach to justifying the "intrinsic thesis" which White critiques is one presented by R. S. Downie, Eileen Loudfoot, and Elizabeth Telfer, in their book *Education and Personal Relationships*. Downie, Loudfoot, and Telfer also reject the "transcendental" justification but they still advocate a justification based on intrinsic grounds: "The simplest justification for education which can be offered–and perhaps the one which in the final showing is the most satisfactory–is that its intrinsic aims, those states of mind which constitute it, are good in themselves or desirable for their own sakes."[7] The reason they give for this intrinsic justification is that "many people, in every age, have claimed it to be so–in other words our appeal is to what would now be called intuition."[8] White is quick to point out that the fact that many people in every age have held the conviction that the possession of knowledge is good in itself "does nothing to show that knowledge-possession *is* good in itself: all these people may have been wrong."[9]

The fourth approach to justifying education based on intrinsic value that White examines is based on Alasdair MacIntyre's article "Against Utilitarianism." MacIntyre argues that:

> Our aim [of education] ought to be to help people to discover activities whose ends are not outside themselves; and it happens to be of the nature of all intellectual inquiry that in and for itself it provides just such activity. The critical ability which ought to be the fruit of education serves nothing directly except for itself, no one except those who exercise it.[10]

White is somewhat sympathetic with MacIntyre's project, but he also thinks that it cannot justify the specific aim MacIntyre has in mind. That is, White agrees with MacIntyre that education should not only be concerned with means to ends, but education should also do something to promote ends in themselves. As White puts it: "[T]here *would* be something irrational if educators only concentrated on means to further means to further means."[11] However, White is quick to point out that although MacIntyre shows that it is a condition of rational behaviour that there be ends-in-themselves, MacIntyre has not given any content to these ends. "In particular, it [MacIntyre's theory] has not identified them [ends] with intellectual pursuits. It emphasizes only the intrinsic nature of these ends."[12]

Thus White concludes his analysis of the possibility of justifying educational activities on intrinsic grounds. In response to White, I would agree with his criticism of Downie, Loudfoot, and Telfer's proposal that education's intrinsic aims, that is, those states of mind which constitute it, are desirable for their own sakes, based on the fact that many people have claimed it to be so, is simply a *fallacy ad populum*. However, the approaches taken by Hirst and Peters, and MacIntyre are not so easily disposed of.

Regarding the transcendental argument utilized by Hirst and Peters, an important distinction must be made between "rationality" and "knowledge." Although Hirst refers to "rational knowledge," these are two distinct concepts; "rationality" having to do with the giving of reasons, and "knowledge" being the "data base" we draw from in giving reasons. The concept of "data base" needs to be expanded somewhat for this analogy to hold. I do not want to include simply "data", but also the connections made between bits of data, that is, what we typically mean when we say that someone understands a body of knowledge. More will be said of the distinction between rationality and knowledge in a following section; however, at this point it is sufficient to note how the distinction helps clarify the intrinsic/instrumental debate. When White, in response to the transcendental argument, counters that the "sceptic is not 'committed to the pursuit of knowledge': the most he is committed to seeking is the specific piece of knowledge which answers his question,"[13] White is referring to knowledge, not rationality. When White argues that the transcendental argument does not show why knowledge is valuable *for its own sake*, "since there is no guarantee that the questioner has not extrinsic reasons for asking his question,"[14] White could very well be correct in suggesting that the questioner has an extrinsic reason for asking his/her question. However, the extrinsic reason the questioner could have would be that the knowledge sought is constitutive of the pursuit of rationality; that is, the acquisition of knowledge is not intrinsic to the educational enterprise, but rather it is constitutive of the pursuit of rationality.[15]

Regarding MacIntyre's argument that education should not be solely concerned with promoting means and that "the critical ability which ought to be the fruit of education serves nothing directly except for itself, no one except those who exercise it,"[16] MacIntyre would appear to be speaking of "rationality" in his reference to "critical ability." White, however, is looking for "knowledge" when he states that "It [MacIntyre's theory] has not given any content, as yet, to these ends."[17] If we separate the "content," that is, knowledge, from the "critical ability," that is, rationality, it would appear that knowledge is not intrinsically justifiable as an educational aim, but rather, it is constitutive of the pursuit of rationality which *is* intrinsically justifiable as an educational aim, in fact, *the* educational aim. However, before presenting this argument, it is important to see how other educational values fit into this "value of rationality" scheme.

Knowledge of Values

In this postmodern age, one cannot assume that the acquisition of knowledge in an educational enterprise is inarguably of fundamental value. The question could easily be raised "is knowledge just one value among other values?" It is important to examine these "other values" and to determine how they fit into a justification for educational activity. Andrew Reid, in an article entitled "Value Pluralism and Physical Education," presents a framework of values derived from philosophers writing in the axiological tradition. He presents what he refers to as a "noncontroversial list of values" which embrace the content and structure of "human well-being or the good life." He provides the following list (in his words, "in no significant order"):

  (i)   the idea of *intellectual or cognitive value*
  (ii)   the idea of *ethical value*
  (iii) the idea of *aesthetic value*
  (iv)   the idea of *economic value*
  (v)   the notion of *hedonic value*
  (vi)   the idea of *health and welfare value.*[18]

Although Reid states that he does not list the values in hierarchical order, he does admit that "where values conflict, we can generally assume that some considerations must be given greater priority."[19] He then proceeds to suggest that "any system of values of the sort which is going to command general *intuitive* agreement is one which acknowledges the overall primacy of ethical considerations."[20] It is interesting to note Reid's use of the term "intuitive agreement" as the basis for accepting a values system. I would argue that the term "rational agreement" would be more fitting. This substitution of terms requires a closer look at what we mean by "intuition." Typically, intuition is set up in opposition to rationality. However, a common characteristic of rational thought and intuitive thought is the utilization of background knowledge; albeit, in the case of intuition, the background knowledge may not be at a conscious level. For example, if someone has a negative intuition, or bad feeling, about a particular place, there are probably similarities between the place under consideration and places where the person has had negative experiences in the past. However, this connection might not be at a conscious level and thus we refer to this feeling as "intuitive." Another example would be that of the chess master who seems to intuit his/her opponent's next move. However the chess master has only become a "master" as a result of a lifetime of games and the knowledge acquired through his/her experience with chess is what makes his/her "intuition" possible.

The importance of background knowledge for both so-called "intuitive" judgements and "rational" judgements would lead me to assert that the acquisition of knowledge is an important value. However, the acquisition of knowledge is not *the* fundamental value as much as the rational thought that requires knowledge. Before presenting this argument, it is important to examine two other alternatives to the "value of knowledge" justification for educational activity.

White, as would Reid, suggests that "[m]ore widespread, perhaps, than the view that education should aim at knowledge for its own sake, is the belief that it should promote the well-being of those who undergo it."[21] White proceeds to argue that "[i]f educators are to aim at promoting the good of their pupils, their work is twofold, partly a matter of enlarging understanding and partly to do with shaping dispositions to behave in certain ways."[22] I would agree whole-heartedly with White's proposition that educators must facilitate the enlarging of their students' understanding of what their well-being consists in. Regarding the other component of the educators' work, that is, shaping dispositions, we must become clear on what is involved in shaping dispositions.

Donald Arnstine reiterates White's claim when he states that "educational aims must shift from the acquisition of knowledge and skills to the acquisition of the dispositions for which those skills are needed."[23] He gives the example of reading. "[A] child will not become a reader unless she becomes disposed to read. A disposition to read can be acquired only if the child enjoys reading or sees some useful purpose in reading."[24] I am not denying the importance of acquiring dispositions in an educational context; however, it is not the dispositions that are fundamental to the educational endeavor, but rather the rational thought necessary for acquiring dispositions. Arnstine suggests two options for acquiring dispositions: the student must come to enjoy the activity under consideration or see the purpose in it. The first option would seem to involve the notion of hedonic value that Reid refers to. The problem with this value, as Reid points out, is that "the only intelligible objection to thinking of pleasure as a component of the good life is the simple observation that some pleasures may be bad for us, may be contrary to our well-being rather than partly constitutive of it."[25] Now I am not implying that reading is a pleasure which is bad for us; however, someone had to make a choice, a rational choice, to include reading as a pleasure which is good for us. Thus, rational thought, the giving of reasons as to why reading should be considered a pleasure which is good for us, must occur before the disposition of reading is instilled in students. The second option Arnstine suggests, that of students seeing the purpose in the activity, likewise requires rational thought. The student must have a conception of means to an end, and this conception must be developed first before students will accept that option for developing a particular disposition. Thus, we see how the development of rationality is a precursor to the development of dispositions.

A final alternative to the "value of knowledge" justification for educational activity is, ironically enough, proposed by Hirst, who, along with Peters, brought the notion of "knowledge intrinsic to education" into the forefront in the 60's. In Hirst's own words: "[W]e must shift from seeing education as primarily concerned with knowledge to seeing it as primarily concerned with social practices."[26] It must be pointed out that Hirst is not denying the importance of reason but he is now emphasizing that reason is not a separate discrete domain. "[O]ur naturally given capacities of reason are exercised from the very start in inextricable involvement in or exerting our other given capacities."[27] Although, the "later Hirst" has been interpreted as jettisoning his previous work on the importance of the forms of knowledge, he is not denying the fundamental importance of rationality. "But the inextricable place of the activities and achievements of reason itself right within and alongside other wants and satisfactions is fundamental to our understanding of ourselves as persons, and to the determination of the good, which is the rational, life for us individually and collectively."[28] The distinction made earlier between rationality and knowledge is important in understanding Hirst's recent work. Although he denies the fundamental importance of initiation into the forms of knowledge (in the theoretical sense he once spoke of, as opposed to the practical knowledge he now refers to), he emphasizes the "practices of critical reflection," which I would understand to mean the practice of rationality, or the giving of reason. "But worthwhile education conceived in these terms requires initiation into the practices of critical reflection on the fundamental substantive practices it basically involves, not merely immersion in these basic practices."[29] Thus, Hirst is not denying, but rather emphasizing, the fundamental importance of rationality as opposed to the fundamental importance of knowledge. It is a more detailed examination of the importance of knowledge in its relation to rationality to which I now turn.

Knowledge and Rationality

In the previous sections, I alluded to a distinction between rationality and knowledge. This distinction was not meant to relegate the acquisition of knowledge to a position of unimportance, but rather to propose that the importance of knowledge lay in its service to rationality. The acquisition of knowledge and understanding provides a context in which rationality can be developed. As put eloquently by Kevin Williams: "[T]he pursuit of scientific understanding offers experiences of wonder, rapture and delight, and provides a context in which rationality and intellectual connoisseurship can be at once exercised and developed."[30] Previously I referred to "knowledge" as the "data base" we draw upon in forming reasons whose formation is fundamental to the concept of rationality. Without this "data base," with what would we reason? Peters emphasizes the importance of a body of knowledge for "critical thought," which I interpret to mean rational thought. "Critical thought, however, is a rationalistic abstraction without a body of knowledge to be critical about."[31]

I must, at this point, extend this concept of a "data base" upon which rational thought requires to operate, to include more than simply propositional knowledge. By expanding our concept of knowledge to include what the later Hirst refers to as "practical knowledge,"[32] as well as the notion that knowledge has a contextual basis, that is, Wittgenstein's notion of language games, we are in a better position to defend the proposal that the acquisition of knowledge is fundamental to the educational enterprise in the sense that it is fundamental for the development of rationality. As C. J. B. MacMillan put it: "[I]t is only when the language-games and world pictures have been acquired that reason can begin. For then the learner is able to ask the questions that lead to the rational teaching modes."[33]

We may even want to push the concept of rationality's "data base" to include what typically falls beyond the scope of "knowledge," for example, intuitions, emotions, and so forth. However, as I proposed earlier, intuitions could be viewed as having a knowledge background, albeit, not at the conscious level. I have argued elsewhere[34] that emotions have rational underpinnings, for example, to experience sadness, one *judges* the situation to merit such feelings. John Colbeck, although he would not necessarily agree with the knowledge base I see as underlying intuitions and emotions, does see the necessity for something upon which reasoning must operate. "We cannot, I think, make sense of any action or conclusion, based on however much reasoning, without reliance on things very much like hunches, instincts, passions and emotional commitments; these are the raw materials without which reasoning could not start."[35] Thus, knowledge, intuitions, emotions, and so forth, are necessary for rationality to operate and their acquisition is important *because* they are needed for rationality to develop. In other words, the development of rationality should be the fundamental value in an educational enterprise and this could not happen without a "data base" to be rational about, so indirectly, knowledge (along with other values, such as intuition and emotion) are important because of their constitutive relationship to the development of rationality. But why should the development of rationality be viewed as the fundamental value of educational experiences? It is to this question we now turn.

Rationality as Intrinsically Valuable

Siegel has provided an admirable defense of rationality against the postmodern tide that many see as destroying any "foundations" found in its path. I cannot hide my affinity for Siegel's work and in advocating the development of rationality as the fundamental value in the educational enterprise, I am heavily indebted to him. I will briefly summarize Siegel's argument and then consider possible alternative positions regarding the value of rationality in the educational arena.

Siegel's first book, *Educating Reason*, is basically a defense of critical thinking as an educational ideal. Siegel does, however, illuminate the intimate connection between critical thinking and rationality.

To be a critical thinker is to be appropriately moved by reasons. To be a rational person is to believe and act on the basis of reasons. There is a deep conceptual connection, by way of the notion of reasons, between critical thinkers and rational persons. Critical thinking is best conceived, consequently, as the *educational cognate* of rationality; critical thinking involves bringing to bear all matters relevant to the rationality of belief and action; and education aimed at the promulgation of critical thinking is nothing less than education aimed at the fostering of rationality and the development of rational persons.[36]

In *Educating Reason*, Siegel provides four reasons for justifying critical thinking as an educational ideal: (i) respect for students as persons, (ii) self-sufficiency and preparation for adulthood, (iii) initiation into the rational traditions, and (iv) critical thinking and democratic living. In his more recent book, *Rationality Redeemed*, Siegel argues:

[T]he fundamental justification for regarding critical thinking as an educational ideal is the first, moral one: conceiving and conducting education in ways which do not take as central the fostering of students' abilities and dispositions to think critically fails to treat students with respect as persons, and so fails to treat them in a morally acceptable way.[37]

Siegel is quick to point out that his justification for critical thinking (and hence, rationality) is obviously "modernist" in its individualistic orientation. We turn now to some of the "postmodern" challenges to the position that rationality should be considered the fundamental value in the educational enterprise.

The most serious objection to the thesis that rationality should be the fundamental value in the educational enterprise concerns the question "is rationality fundamentally valuable or is it a value among other equally valuable alternatives?" Siegel sets out this problem by considering the substantive versus contextual nature of rationality.

[S]ome writers who favor educational ideals associated with "reason" argue that this ideal must be understood not only substantively, but also contextually. The suggestion here is not only that contextual considerations are highly relevant to determining what, in a given context, it is rational to believe, judge or do–with this I agree–but also that what rationality is, the very substance of this notion, is itself contextually determined, so that rationality itself–as a concept, and, therefore, as an educational ideal–is contextually bound, and alters from context to context.[38]

Siegel considers Nicholas Burbules's "contextualism" and Burbules's proposal that "[t]o be reasonable in social contexts of interaction entails remaining open to the influences of other avenues [than that of the force of reasons] of mutual exploration, negotiation, and the pursuit of understanding."[39] Siegel responds by agreeing that we should remain open to such influences but he raises the question concerning when we should allow and when we should resist such influences.

> Without recourse to standards which (fallibly) help us to sort out the legitimate from the illegitimate influences–the ones which ought to move us (because they provide good reason to believe, judge or act in a particular way) from the ones whose influence we ought to resist (because they fail to provide such reason)–there is no way to secure the judgment that in a given case our being influenced is/was in fact reasonable. That is, regarding some belief, judgment or action as reasonable requires that we appeal to something other than the process through which the judgment was reached.[40]

In suggesting that there are standards which could be considered universal, albeit fallible, to which we can appeal to in making judgments, Siegel has come under fire by postmodernists who claim that we must embrace the particular, not the universal. Siegel examines Richard Rorty's exclusive and exhaustive distinction between particularity and universality and Rorty's rejection of "objectivity"–the view that as philosophical inquirers we must "step outside our community long enough to examine it in the light of something which transcends it, namely, that which it has in common with every other actual and possible community" and Rorty's embracement of "solidarity"–"we must, in practice, privilege our own group, even though there can be no non-circular justification for doing so."[41] Siegel does not accept the thesis that the universal and the particular are incompatible as implied by Rorty's distinction between objectivity and solidarity. Siegel accepts the fact that humans are always located in specific cultural/historical settings but he argues that this does not undermine people's collective ability to reach beyond local settings and speak to broader audiences. "If *all* of our judgments are made from the perspective of whatever scheme we happen to employ–which they are–then, according to that argument [the argument that our judgments cannot have any force beyond the bounds of our own location or scheme], *none* of them has any such legitimacy."[42] But Siegel proceeds to point out numerous counterexamples: mathematical judgments which from our scheme have legitimacy, but which small children and members of certain other cultures do not share, for example, ancient Greeks before the invention/discovery of irrational numbers or nineteenth century geometers before the discovery of non-Euclidean geometries; scientific discoveries beyond the scheme of those who invented them, for example, space "curves" or mass as convertible with energy; or, moral judgments such as the judgment that oppression and marginalization are wrong.[43] Thus, Siegel demonstrates that the argument that our judgments cannot have any force beyond the bounds of our own location or scheme is a *non sequitur*.

Although I agree with Siegel's counter-arguments concerning the legitimacy of judgments which go beyond the bounds of our own locations and schemes, I find the most convincing argument against postmodern attacks, for example, attacks against "metanarratives," attacks against the "maleness" of rationality, and so forth, to be an argument of logic; that is, one could not argue for the deconstruction of "metanarratives" or the inclusion of "female voices" without recourse to reason, hence rationality. In Siegel's words: "To say that all metanarratives are to be rejected, that they are all defective, is to make a universalizing claim of exactly the sort that the person making the claim wants to (universally) reject. But if rejecting metanarratives requires embracing a metanarrative, then there is a logical difficulty inherent in the very idea of rejecting them all."[44] Regarding the feminist critique of rationality, Siegel reiterates the logical argument: "[O]ne cannot reject all standards, and the very possibility of evaluation, and at the same time embrace philosophical feminism as an ideal or as a standard of evaluation of discourses and/or theories."[45] Until someone is able to present an alternative to rationality, not using rational thought in the process, it would appear that rationality should be considered the fundamental value in an educational enterprise, since evaluation of all other educational values relies on the possibility of giving reasons for one value as opposed to another value.

Implications for Education

I began this chapter by examining the notion of "knowledge intrinsic to education"–a notion made popular by Hirst and Peters in the '60s but whose remnants remain evident today when the acquisition of knowledge is espoused as a justification for educational experiences. However, it is not the acquisition of knowledge which is intrinsically valuable since knowledge should be viewed as constitutive of the development of rationality, which should be the fundamental value of the educational enterprise, since rational thought was required to get the "values of education" project off the ground. The implications of this view for educational practice is not the abandonment of the aim of acquiring knowledge, but rather, the expansion of what we mean by knowledge. Since the development of rationality requires the ability to give reasons, the wider a student's "data base" from which to draw upon, the greater the possibility of arriving at *good* reasons. Some may argue that the giving of reasons is a "quality not quantity" situation, but even if a student arrives at a good reason without working through many alternatives, having a wide data base of alternatives would be helpful in confirming the appropriateness of the reason given. Thus, not only would the acquisition of Hirst's traditional forms of knowledge be important in developing a data base for rational thought; but also the acquisition of practical knowledge, for example, physical education activities; and knowledge connected more intimately with the affective domain, for example, aesthetic activities, in the sense of Peter Abbs's "sensuous understanding."[46] In conclusion then, an expansion of the concept of "knowledge" to include other values is important in the educational enterprise because a wide base of knowledge is instrumental for the development of rationality, which I have argued, is intrinsic to the very justification of any values, not the least of these, educational values.

Chapter 3

The Fundamental Role of Critical Thinking in Physical Education and Sport

In arguing for the inclusion of physical education in the educational curriculum based on the potential for students to acquire practical knowledge through participation in physical activities, I advocated Carr's basis of assessment for practical knowledge situations. He suggests that for one to know how to do x, one must 1) entertain $x$ing as a purpose, 2) be acquainted with a set of practical procedures for successful $x$ing, and 3) exhibit recognizable success at $x$ing. Condition 1), entertaining $x$ing as a purpose, involves the notion of intentionality discussed in chapter one. In this chapter, I want to examine condition 2) and demonstrate how being acquainted with a set of practical procedures for successful $x$ing involves critical thinking, and thus demonstrate how critical thinking is fundamental to physical education and sport. Condition 3), exhibiting recognizable success at $x$ing will be examined in chapter four. Before considering the role played by critical thinking in physical education and sport, it is important that I first clarify what is involved in critical thinking as well as provide a justification for why we should even be concerned that students become critical thinkers.

What is Critical Thinking?

Critical thinking has been conceived of both in a broad and narrow sense. In its broad sense, critical thinking has been conceived of as thinking critically or finding fault with particular thoughts or positions. Besides exhibiting an obvious circularity, this conception does not adequately convey the rigorous judgement involved in critical thinking. On the other end of the spectrum, we have a much narrower conception of critical thinking as thinking equated with informal logic. Richard Paul gives these opposing conceptions a temporal flavor by suggesting that the "first wave" of the critical thinking movement involved a "logical core" and that the field during this wave (1964-1980) was dominated primarily by philosophers with an expertise in logic. Paul argues that, although the philosophers gave the domain of critical thinking an intellectual foundation, they did not go far enough in identifying the variables which play a role in thinking, such as intuition, emotion, and the contextualization of critical thinking. Paul describes the "second wave" of the critical thinking movement as occurring from 1980-1994 and he suggests that this wave involved a much broader approach in that proponents outside of the disciplines of logic and philosophy began dealing with some of the variables missed in the first wave. However, because these attempts were uncoordinated and were coming from many different disciplines, for example, psychology, business, and education (often with no background in first wave theory), the work produced was of mixed quality. Paul suggests that the "third wave" is just now emerging and that this wave represents a commitment to avoid the weaknesses of the first two waves, that is, to include both rigour and comprehensiveness.[1] We will now consider the works of some of the critical thinking theorists who would be considered "third wave".

Although there exists a myriad of definitions of critical thinking, we will limit ourselves to the works of what Ralph Johnson refers to as "the group of five"–Robert Ennis, Richard Paul, Matthew Lipman, Harvey Siegel, and John McPeck.[2] These five theorists have not simply stated isolated definitions of critical thinking but rather have proposed concepts, principles, arguments, and assumptions which support particular definitions. After explicating and critiquing these five conceptions of critical thinking, I will turn to the question of whether critical thinking is generalizable or subject-specific.

Ennis is typically credited with bringing the critical thinking topic to the forefront with his 1962 article "A Concept of Critical Thinking" published in the *Harvard Educational Review*. In this article, he defines critical thinking as "the correct assessing of statements" and then considers twelve aspects of critical thinking, such as "grasping the meaning of a statement, judging whether there is ambiguity in a line of reasoning, judging whether certain statements contradict each other," and so forth.[3] A criticism of Ennis's original definition of critical thinking was that it was purely skill oriented; that is, if a student mastered the twelve aspects of critical thinking, he/she would meet the definition of being a critical thinker. However, this conception did not address the necessity of actually utilizing these skills. In response to the criticism concerning the disposition to utilize critical thinking skills, Ennis revised his definition in a 1987 article entitled "A Taxonomy of Critical Thinking Dispositions and Abilities." In this article, he defines critical thinking as "reasonable reflective thinking that is focused on deciding what to believe or do" and he includes not only abilities, such as "identifying or formulating a question, analyzing arguments, asking and answering questions of clarification, judging the credibility of a source," and so forth, but he also includes fourteen dispositions, such as "seeking a clear statement of the thesis or question, seeking reasons, trying to be well informed, using and mentioning credible sources," and so forth.[4]

Paul acknowledges the importance of the disposition to utilize critical thinking skills and abilities. The emphasis he places on such a disposition is evident in the distinction he makes between critical thinking in the "strong" and "weak" sense. Paul suggests that:

> As we come to habitually think critically in the strong sense we develop special *traits of mind*: intellectual humility, intellectual courage, intellectual perseverance, intellectual integrity, and confidence in reason. A sophistic or weak sense critical thinker develops these traits only in a restricted way, consistent with egocentric and sociocentric commitments.[5]

In other words, not only must critical thinkers utilize critical thinking skills, if they are to think critically in a *strong sense*, they must apply these skills to their *own* positions. If critical thinkers remain at the weak sense stage, they become, in Paul's words, "[M]ore sophistic rather than less so, more skilled in 'rationalizing' and 'intellectualizing' the biases they already have."[6]

Criticisms which could be levied against Paul's distinction between strong and weak senses of critical thinking include: 1) that the distinction is difficult to make, and 2) that weak sense critical thinking may not be critical thinking after all. Regarding the first criticism, Siegel questions how we are to distinguish between instances where egocentrism, sociocentrism, and self-deception are manifest and where they are not. He cites the example of the difficulty in distinguishing between the biologist who believes that lung cancer is caused by a virus because she is convinced by the experimental evidence, and the biologist who believes it because the originator of the theory is a personal idol or mentor.[7] The second criticism involves questioning whether weak sense critical thinking is actually critical thinking. Paul himself refers to critical thinking as being "disciplined, self-directed thinking which exemplifies the perfections of thinking appropriate to a particular mode or domain of thinking."[8] One of the perfections which Paul cites is that of consistency. If one of the requirements for critical thinking is consistency, then it is questionable whether weak sense critical thinking should be considered critical thinking since the thinker is exhibiting non-consistency in not applying critical thinking skills to his or her own position.

Lipman emphasizes the importance of applying critical thinking to one's own position when he suggests that critical thinking is self-correcting. He argues that critical thinking is "thinking that (1) facilitates judgment because it (2) relies on criteria, (3) is self-correcting, and (4) is sensitive to context."[9] The criteria which Lipman suggests we must teach children to recognize and use include: standards, laws, precepts, conventions, principles, ideals, tests, methods, and so forth. In utilizing such criteria, Lipman acknowledges the importance of being sensitive to context and this involves recognizing: exceptional or irregular circumstances; special limitations, contingencies, or constraints; overall configurations; the possibility that evidence is atypical; and the possibility that some meanings do not translate from one context or domain to another.[10]

Although Lipman specifies properties of critical thinking, he has been criticized as not really providing necessary and sufficient conditions for someone to be classified as a critical thinker. Paul suggests that one could find instances of thinking that were self-correcting, used criteria, and responded to context in one sense and nevertheless were uncritical in some other sense. One's criteria might be uncritically chosen or the manner of responding to context might be critically deficient.[11] In fairness to Lipman, in a more recent publication he acknowledged that "[a]nother consideration is that we have *standards* of acceptability for each criterion, indicating the degree to which each criterion is to be satisfied if the thinking in question is to be considered acceptable."[12] Another interesting counter-example suggested by Johnson concerns the person who is good at self-correction, for example, looking critically at one's own beliefs, theories, and so forth, but is highly resistant to criticism from others.

This person would seem to be missing a feature necessary for one to be referred to as a critical thinker.[13]

Siegel proposes a conception of critical thinking that involves what he considers to be two necessary and sufficient conditions: 1) reason assessment, and 2) a critical spirit. Regarding reason assessment, Siegel argues that "a critical thinker must be able to assess reasons and their ability to warrant beliefs, claims and actions properly. This means that the critical thinker must have a good understanding of, and the ability to utilize, principles governing the assessment of reasons."[4] Concerning the critical spirit, Siegel proposes that "a critical thinker is, in addition, a certain sort of person. Dispositions, inclinations, habits of mind, character traits–these features of the critical thinker are present, and definitive of the critical thinker, even when they are not being utilized or acted upon." Thus, Siegel defines a critical thinker as someone "who is appropriately moved by reasons."[15]

Siegel's connection between reasons and principles involving consistency, impartiality, non-arbitrariness, and so forth, has come under attack from those in the postmodern philosophical camp. Closely tied to this emphasis on principled reasoning is the connection between critical thinking and rationality. In fact, Siegel argues:

> [C]ritical thinking is best conceived, consequently, as the *educational cognate* of rationality; critical thinking involves bringing to bear all matters relevant to the rationality of belief and action; and education aimed at the promulgation of critical thinking is nothing less than education aimed at the fostering of rationality and the development of rational persons.[17]

When Siegel refers to the development of rational persons, some feminist philosophers have questioned whether these persons include both male and female. I have argued elsewhere[18] that the feminist critique levied against the traditional conception of rationality demonstrates the employment of reason assessment and a critical attitude. The utilization by feminist philosophers of the intellectual tools of which they are critical, may suggest that principled reasoning is not masculine but rather part of what it means to be human. Although we cannot go into more detail concerning a critique of the concept of rationality at this point, a discussion of issues relating to rationality and knowledge will be resumed in the section on a justification for the teaching of critical thinking.

McPeck, in his conception of critical thinking, raises an issue that has not yet specifically been addressed in the preceding discussion concerning definitions of critical thinking. This issue concerns the subject-specificity of critical thinking. McPeck is critical of the possibility of generalizing critical thinking skills. "It is a matter of conceptual truth that thinking is always thinking about X, and that X can never be 'everything in general' but must always be something in particular. Thus the claim 'I teach my students to think' is at worst false and at best misleading."[19]

If McPeck's thesis is correct, the implications for education are significant. However, McPeck has been criticized for committing a fundamental error in his reasoning. As Seigel points out, McPeck confuses thinking generally (i.e., as denoting a *type* of activity) with specific *acts* (i.e., tokens) or instances of thinking. Seigel suggests that:

> It is not the case that the general activity of thinking "is logically connected to an X," any more than the general activity of cycling is logically connected to any particular bicycle. It is true that any given act of cycling must be done on some bicycle or other. But it surely does not follow that the general activity of cycling cannot be discussed independently of any particular bicycle.[20]

Paul reiterates this criticism by suggesting the counter-example of writing. "Certainly most can see the fallacy in inferring that, because one cannot write without writing about something, some specific subject or other, it is therefore unintelligible 'muddled nonsense' to maintain general composition courses."[21]

Having explicated and critiqued, albeit briefly, the conceptions of critical thinking proposed by Ennis, Paul, Lipman, Siegel, and McPeck, I would argue that Siegel's "appropriately moved by reasons"[22] conception encompasses the conceptions of the other four theorists. Ennis's revised conception of critical thinking as "reasonable [i.e., having to do with reasons] reflective thinking that is focused on deciding what to believe or do"[23] includes a list of abilities and dispositions, both of which are considered by Siegel to be necessary and sufficient conditions for someone to be considered a critical thinker. The necessity of skills and dispositions is also evident in Paul's conception of "strong sense" critical thinking when he proposes that "in thinking critically we use our command of *the elements of thinking* [skills]" and "as we come to habitually think critically in the strong sense we develop special *traits of mind* [dispositions]."[24]

Although Lipman's properties of critical thinking, that is, "thinking which relies on criteria, is self-correcting, and is sensitive to context,"[25] do not come across as necessary and sufficient conditions, the ability to recognize and utilize criteria and context could be viewed as a skill (although "appropriate" would have to be added to the kinds of criteria relied upon if this conception was to be accepted by Siegel). The property of self-correction, if understood as being synonymous with self-critical, would fall under Paul's "strong sense" critical thinking and would demonstrate the disposition condition included in Siegel's conception. McPeck's conception of critical thinking as "having the disposition and skill to do X [any problem or activity requiring some mental effort] in such a way that E [available evidence from the pertinent field or problem area], or some subset of E, is suspended as being sufficient to establish the truth or viability of P [some proposition or action within X]"[26] is encompassed by Siegel's "moved by reasons" conception, except for the emphasis on the subject-specificity of X.

Before concluding our discussion of what we mean by critical thinking, it is important to consider the implications of this discussion for the areas of physical education. By arguing that critical thinking involves skills and the disposition to utilize these skills [i.e., the critical spirit] in reason assessment, and by suggesting that, along with the generalizable critical spirit and the underlying epistemology concerning reason assessment, critical thinking involves subject-specific content knowledge, the path has been paved for an argument in support of the role of critical thinking in physical education. If a totally generalist approach was taken, critical thinking skills and dispositions would be taught separately from specific course content, for example, a critical thinking course. By acknowledging the importance of subject-specific content knowledge, it becomes feasible to teach critical thinking within a subject area, either explicitly or implicitly [what Ennis refers to as the "infusion" or "immersion" approach, respectively[27]]. Although the physical education class is not typically viewed as an important arena for the development of critical thinking skills and dispositions, I will argue in the following sections that, on the contrary, critical thinking has a *fundamental* role to play in physical education.

Why Teach Critical Thinking?

Although physical education theorists are beginning to recognize the role of critical thinking in physical education,[28] justification for the teaching of critical thinking has received minimal attention. I will first consider a justification for the teaching of critical thinking generally and then present an argument for the teaching of critical thinking in the context of physical education specifically.

I propose that the most convincing argument for justifying the teaching of critical thinking is an argument based on respect for the autonomy of persons. A seminal work concerning autonomy is the work of Immanuel Kant. One Kantian principle is that we treat others as ends and not means. In Kant's own words:

> The ground of this principle is: rational nature exists as an end in itself. Man necessarily thinks of his own existence in this way; thus far it is a subjective principle of human actions. Also every other rational being thinks of his existence by means of the same rational ground which holds also for myself, thus it is at the same time an objective principle from which, as a supreme practical ground, it must be possible to derive all laws of the will. The practical imperative, therefore, is the following: Act so that you treat humanity, whether in your own person or in that of another, always as an end and never as a means.[29]

This principle involves recognizing the worth of all persons as the basis for respecting all persons. As Kant states: "[A]utonomy is the basis of the dignity of both human nature and every rational nature."[30] This respect for persons as autonomous agents includes respect for students; that is, students should be treated with the respect every autonomous agent is deserving of. Respecting this autonomy involves, as Seigel points out, recognizing the students' right to exercise independent judgement and powers of evaluation.[31] If students are to exercise independent judgement, these judgements should be sound. The exercising of sound judgements require the development of critical thinking skills and dispositions. For example, skills and dispositions such as Ennis's (1987) "seeking reasons, trying to be well informed, judging the credibility of a source," and so forth[32] are necessary for making sound judgements. Without these skills and the disposition to use them, students (or anyone, for that matter) would make unfounded judgements or judgements based on fallacious reasons or inaccurate information.

A secondary argument, which is closely related to the argument based on the respect for students as persons, concerns education's task of preparing students for adulthood. In Seigel's words, "[E]ducation strives to enable children to face adulthood successfully. In particular, we hope that education fosters in children the power and ability to control, insofar as they are able, their own lives."[33] Siegel suggests that in order for students to have control over their own lives, they must be self-sufficient. "[S]uch a person is free from the unwarranted and undesirable control of unjustified beliefs, unsupportable attitudes, and paucity of abilities, which can prevent that person from competently taking charge of her own life."[34] Having the skills and dispositions necessary to justify beliefs and attitudes is part of what it means to be a critical thinker. By *justifying* beliefs and attitudes, we are referring to providing good reasons for such beliefs and attitudes. The necessity of providing *good reasons* avoids the possibility of rationalizing some immoral belief or attitude since such a belief or attitude would not be able to withstand counter-arguments which provide better reasons for not holding such a belief or attitude. Being able to respond to counter-arguments is an important ability for students to acquire if they want to be critical thinkers. An important question must be dealt with at this point; if we are trying to help students become autonomous agents, what if they say they do not want to be critical thinkers? Teachers can respond to such a position by asking students why they do not want to be critical thinkers. As soon as students start providing reasons for their choice, the teacher should point out that they are engaging in critical thinking. However, the teacher does not want to leave the situation at students exhibiting critical thinking, he/she wants to help students develop into *good* critical thinkers.

Having considered justificatory arguments for the teaching of critical thinking generally, we turn now to the teaching of critical thinking in the context of physical education specifically. The argument concerning self-sufficiency would appear to be particularly relevant in the realm of physical education. Physical education is an area where, among other concerns, issues of health, physical fitness, and lifetime leisure pursuits are frequently addressed. If we want students to competently take charge of their own lives, they will have to make decisions concerning health, fitness, leisure pursuits, and so forth. In order to make these decisions competently, students require critical thinking skills and dispositions. It must also be pointed out that if the above mentioned arguments for justifying critical thinking generally are accepted, an argument would have to be presented to justify the *exclusion* of teaching critical thinking in physical education. In the absence of such an argument, there would seem to be no reason to exclude the teaching of critical thinking in physical education (or any

other specific subject, for that matter). One possible argument against
the teaching of critical thinking in physical education could be
advocated by someone conceiving of physical education as involving
strictly disciplined physical training. However, we would make a
distinction between training and education in this example, and argue
that education is broader than training, and thus, for the reasons
mentioned previously, an emphasis on critical thinking is justified.

Taking a more proactive approach, teaching critical thinking in
physical education could be justified from a pragmatic perspective. In
a time of cost-cutting and the back-to-basics movement, physical
educators are having to justify their subject's position in the school
curriculum. By demonstrating the potential for teaching critical
thinking in the physical education class, physical educators could take
the line that such a possibility demonstrates a similarity between
physical education and what are typically considered more academic
subjects. However, such an approach is actually counter-productive in
its attempt to justify a position for physical education in the curriculum.
By stressing how the possibility of teaching critical thinking in physical
education makes physical education more like other subjects, physical
educators are leaving themselves open to the counter-argument that
rather than including physical education because it is like other
subjects, schools could simply just include the other subjects.

A much stronger argument for the justification of physical education
in the school curriculum does not rely on its similarity with other
subjects, but rather on its uniqueness. While most subjects in the
school curriculum involve the acquisition of theoretical knowledge,
physical education is one of few subjects whose focus is on practical as
well as theoretical knowledge. As argued in chapter one, providing the
opportunity to develop practical as well as theoretical knowledge is
important if we want to develop all facets of our students' potentials.
As mentioned in the beginning of this chapter, critical thinking is an
integral component of the development of practical knowledge. Recall
Carr's second condition for the assessment of practical knowledge
situations. The second condition, being acquainted with a set of
practical procedures for successful *x*ing, is analogous to providing a
justification for a theoretical knowledge claim.   Providing a
justification is central to what it means to be moved by reasons [recall
Siegel's conception of critical thinking explicated in the first section of
this chapter]. To clarify what he means by "being acquainted with a set
of practical procedures for successful *x*ing," Carr revives Aristotle's

notion of practical inference: It is *A*'s purpose to *x*; *A* understands that *y*ing is a satisfactory way to *x*; *A y*s.

> Such a form of inference offers us a way to demonstrate just how simple or basic actions from which complicated skills are built—relate to one another as means to ends. In general, then, there is no more reason to deny that relations of a logical kind may hold between the characterisations of the individual actions that are parts of the complicated patterns of activity that are exercises of knowing how, than there is to deny that such relations also hold between the descriptions of the judgments that offer logical or evidential support for a given bit of knowing that.[35]

Just as recognizing and utilizing logical or evidential support for "knowing that" is what is entailed in critical thinking, so too is the recognition and utilization of individual actions to achieve success in the more complicated patterns of activity of which achievement is considered an act of "knowing how" entailed in critical thinking. It must be noted at this point that to recognize and utilize individual actions to achieve success in more complicated patterns of activity does not necessarily require the ability to verbalize this connection. One often has to perform the movement in an attempt to explain how the pattern is achieved. However, a "physical" explanation of a movement pattern does not negate the provision of support that is analogous to the provision of evidential support for instances of theoretical knowledge. Thus, if one accepts the practical knowledge argument in support of the inclusion of physical education in the curriculum, a strong justification for critical thinking has been achieved.

How Do We Teach Critical Thinking?

Having provided a series of justificatory arguments in support of the teaching of critical thinking generally and in a physical education context specifically, I turn now to an examination of how critical thinking could be fostered (directly and indirectly) through physical education. If one considers the typical physical education program, it frequently entails the teaching of games (including specific sports in the higher grades), educational gymnastics (usually in the lower grades), and dance. Besides these "practical knowledge" areas, the physical education program also typically includes the more "theoretical knowledge" areas encompassing physical health, fitness, anatomy, and so forth. I will examine each of these areas and provide practical suggestions as to how critical thinking could be fostered through them.

The teaching and playing of games and sports is ripe with the opportunity for the teaching and utilization of critical thinking. Both in the learning of basic movement skills as well as specific sport skills, and in the playing of sports and games, critical thinking has a fundamental role to play. However, the critical thinking aspect of learning skills and playing games is not always emphasized by the teacher. Regarding the teaching of basic movement skills, Fran Cleland and Cynthia Pearse suggest having students experiment with various components of particular movement skills such as throwing, that is, preparation movements, wind-up, release point, or follow-through.[36] They suggest asking students to describe which components help to produce force, determine direction, determine height and distance, and so forth. In describing which components affect the movements and how, the students are providing reasons for particular movements. This provision of reasons, as argued earlier, is an integral part of critical thinking.

Using more of a movement education approach to teaching movement skills, Cleland and Pearse suggest asking students to generate various ways to bounce, kick, or catch a ball in their own space. They suggest changing the conditions of the task so that students must determine how to modify the skill to meet the demands of the task. The students must use previous information, compare and contrast, make inferences, and subsequently select movement solutions which would be most effective within the given conditions. Finding the most effective movement solutions is important for developing competency in skills that will later be used in various sports and games. Movement education is an approach commonly used in early years physical education programs.[37] This approach is particularly conducive to the utilization of the critical thinking skills and dispositions involved in reason assessment.

Once children have learned the necessary basic movement skills, these skills can be utilized in game situations. There are a number of ways in which playing low-organized games can help foster critical thinking. Robert Hautala gives the example of an already designed game which the teacher lets the students play and then asks the students if they have any modifications they could suggest which might make the game better, emphasizing why these modifications would improve the game. He suggests beginning with a simple game with a few obvious difficulties and then progressing through problems of increasing complexity and subtlety.[38] Although modifying a game in such a way could occur in the classroom, the advantage of conducting this activity in the gymnasium is that the students could "test" their modifications by playing the game at various stages. Students can also design their own games. Cleland and Pearse suggest having the teacher provide some criteria or rules for a game. Then the students determine equipment, number of players, rules, object of the game, boundaries, and players' roles.[39] If the designing of games is to help students develop critical thinking skills and dispositions, students should be asked to explain/defend why their game fits the given criteria.

Students in the higher grades are typically taught sport specific skills that are then utilized in sport situations. Critical thinking plays an important role in learning specific sport skills.

> For example, learning to serve a tennis ball requires the learner to be able to analyze the movements involved, compare/contrast his or her performance attempts with a model, sequence movements (swing of the racket with the toss of the ball) appropriately, predict where the ball will land in the opponent's court, decide if the serve was successful, and evaluate the effectiveness of the trial in preparation for future attempts.[40]

Critical thinking is necessary not only for learning sport skills but also for using these skills in a game situation.

> [I]n a sport such as soccer wherein the contextual circumstances involve a moving ball as well as a dispositional fluidity of players, skillfulness, at the highest level, is not so much recognized by the ability to trap, dribble, head, and lay-off the ball competently, though these skills remain important, as by an ability to utilize these acquired learnings intelligently as the game is being played. These separately acquired skills will only be of use if they serve in the development and promotion of tactical procedures and dynamic strategies.[41]

Although it is quite challenging to teach students skills and games emphasizing critical thinking, the payoff in the long run will be the development of more proficient players as well as thinkers. Techniques which can be used to analyze movements, compare and contrast performance attempts, evaluate effectiveness, and so forth, include watching game films, participating in practice drills and scrimmages, as well as participating in game experiences.

Having considered how critical thinking can be fostered through the teaching and playing of games and sports, I will now examine the potential for teaching critical thinking in other areas of the physical education program. Both educational gymnastics and dance involve a large degree of divergent movement and this situation lends itself to the development of critical thinking skills. Cleland and Pearse suggest some educational gymnastics activities that require critical thinking. One activity involves having a student execute a symmetrical shape and/or balance. Another student attempts to change some aspect of that shape or balance so that it becomes asymmetrical. Students must then defend their movement solutions by providing reasons for their choices. Another example involves having students design movement sequences using selected pieces of equipment. Students can be asked to incorporate changes in direction, on/off movements, changes in speed, and transfer of weight on different body parts.[42] In choosing particular movements, students are having to consider alternatives and justify one choice over another. These aspects of critical thinking may not be evident to the students unless the teacher gives feedback, asking for the reasons the students chose a particular movement as opposed to another.

Dance activities that require critical thinking include providing students with other artistic stimuli, for example, poetry, music, visual art, and having students analyze the movement potential within the stimulus art form. Students would be asked to express the movement potential in the art form with their bodies. Another dance activity that requires critical thinking involves providing students with an idea, feeling, or image, and having them choose movements that convey this idea, feeling, or image. In both activities, students should be asked to justify why they chose particular movements in their expression of the stimulus art form or idea, feeling or image.

Besides the "practical knowledge" areas of games/sports, gymnastics and dance, the physical education program also typically includes the more "theoretical knowledge" areas encompassing physical health, fitness, anatomy, and so forth. Although it may be more obvious how critical thinking can be fostered in these theoretical as opposed to practical areas, it would still seem fruitful to cite a few specific examples concerning critical thinking and the theoretical knowledge areas in physical education. Karen Greenockle and Gracie Purvis point out:

With the critical thinking approach, students are encouraged to reason about their fitness and health behaviors; reach conclusions about past, present, and future habits; examine implications of poor versus good fitness/health behaviors; and practice decision-making skills regarding their own fitness and health.[43]

Specific examples utilizing a critical thinking approach include having students look through newspapers, magazines, pamphlets, and videos to compare similarities and differences of their beliefs about fitness and its benefits and those of the experts.[44] A discussion could also be held on issues such as body-building supplements.

"What exactly is the claim made by the body-building supplement?" you ask your students. "What are the reasons for believing it? What reasons might there be *against* believing it?" As students offer their ideas, you encourage them to support their reasons with evidence.[45]

In order that students have a good basis from which to evaluate particular claims, teachers must provide basic logic and reasoning skills, appropriate to the age level of the students. These skills would include looking at ambiguous meanings, possible contradictory evidence, fallacies, and so forth.

Although I have only provided a few examples demonstrating the potential for critical thinking in both the practical and theoretical knowledge areas of physical education, these examples should be sufficient to convince physical educators that there are numerous opportunities in the physical education context for the fostering of critical thinking skills and dispositions.

Chapter 4

The Fundamental Role of Competition in Physical Education and Sport

In chapter three, I argued that critical thinking plays a fundamental role in physical education and sport. This argument was based on Carr's second condition for the assessment of practical knowledge conditions. As alluded to in chapter three, I now want to examine Carr's third condition; that is, exhibiting recognizable success at *x*ing. I will argue that exhibiting recognizable success at *x*ing can best be accomplished through competitive activities. However, this suggestion will come under attack from educators who view competition as a negative thing. Thus, I will first have to consider the negative and positive views of competition.

Competition: Positive or Negative?

> [C]ompetition in sport is, in essence, an expression of friendship, mutuality, goodwill, in which we pay each other the high compliment of offering each other our best opposition to provide for ourselves and the other the satisfaction found in striving to do one's best.[1]

> Ironically, people are being destroyed by an extension of their own competitive ethic. They know their game of football, their game of politics, their game of life. Win in any way you can. The wholesale subscription to this principle motivates the most "savage" acts of our time. Assassins, terrorists, warriors, and war makers are not "crazy," they have merely brought *the win-at-all-costs* dictum whole-heartedly.[2]

The above quotations epitomize the extreme positions people have taken regarding their conceptions of competition. What should be made of such opposing views of the virtues and vices of competition? Is participation in competitive activities a positive or a negative thing? To determine whether participation in competitive activities should be encouraged or discouraged, arguments in support and arguments against competition must be considered.

In arguing for or against the value of competition, a distinction must be made between values *resulting* from participation in an act of competition and values that are *intrinsic* to the concept of competition. Values resulting from participation in an act of competition are not intrinsic to the nature of competition in that these values may or may not occur and if they do occur, they may be the result of factors other than the act of competition. However, values that are intrinsic to the concept of competition will always occur when competition takes place because these values are included among the defining characteristics of what it means to compete.

The Positive View of Competition

Various arguments have extolled the virtues of competition. The suggestion that values can be acquired as a *result* of participating in competitive activities such as sports is best summed up in the often touted cliche "sports build character." Character traits whose development have been attributed to participation in competitive activities include courage, dedication, discipline, perseverance, and so forth. Participation in competitive activities has also been expounded as being a necessary preparation for life. That is, western society is highly competitive and thus the suggestion has been put forth that early competitive experiences will provide the skills and attitudes necessary to compete in this society.

Eleanor Metheny suggests that "for the competitor, the *intrinsic* value of competition is found in the act of competing–the striving, the doing, the satisfaction of using himself fully within the limits of the situation (italics added)."[3] Drew Hyland emphasizes the striving together which is evident in the root word *com-petitio* (to question together, to strive together). "It is a questioning of each other *together*, a striving *together*, presumably so that each participant achieves a level of excellence that could not have been achieved alone, without the mutual striving, without the competition."[4] Robert Simon proposes that when such competition is engaged in voluntarily as "a *mutually* acceptable quest for excellence through challenge (italics added),"[5] then its position is ethically defensible.

The Negative View of Competition

Once again, a distinction must be made between the negative consequences that could *result* from participating in competitive activities and the suggestion that competition is *intrinsically* negative. A potentially negative consequence of competitive activities results from the generation of inequalities. In Simon's words, "[I]t [competition] divides us into winners and losers, successes and failures, stars and scrubs."[6] It is the fact that "someone has to lose" which has led many educators to criticize participation in competitive activities. If participants in competitive activities are continuously losing, a "self-fulfilling prophecy" often results and these participants will drop out, feeling that they can never win. Of course, this situation works both ways–participants who continuously win will be motivated to keep playing. However, it is the situation of the losers which is focused upon by those holding a negative view of competition. Hollis Fait and John Billing suggest that "we must work against any situation which produces large numbers of failures and thus expectations of failure. Possibly then we can stop our unintentional, but nevertheless detrimental, division of students into winners and losers."[7] A point could be made here that if there is a large number of failures, the losers feel "average" and the winners feel "good" as opposed to the situation where there is a small number of failures and the losers feel "bad" and the winners feel "average".[8] However, Fait and Billing advocate against a situation where losers feel bad at worst and only average at best.

Other negative consequences that could result from participation in competitive activities are related to the "win at all costs" attitude that often accompanies the act of competing. In the drive to win, many participants have resorted to cheating. Cheating occurs in many forms, including intentional fouls and intentional injuries. The "win at all costs" attitude might not always result in the extreme consequence of cheating but the price paid in participants' drive to win might be the sacrifice of their individual identities, their education or their health. Some critics feel that involvement in competitive activities may not only limit the educational opportunities of participants, but that competition and education are actually antithetical. In David Campbell's words, "Kids in our society may always engage in some competition, but it is not the teacher's job to promote it, for it has nothing to do with education."[9] Steve Grineski suggests that "[c]ompetition is a noneducational practice for children: an exclusive, not inclusive, practice that limits learning opportunities for most students."[10]

Besides the negative consequences of inequalities, cheating, and the potential tension with educational opportunities, some critics of competitive activities have suggested that competition is intrinsically negative.[11] As Alfie Kohn points out: "[W]e must recognize that the problem rests squarely with the structure of mutually exclusive goal attainment. We need not know anything about the individuals involved to see the destructive potential of a system that says only one of them can be successful."[12] M. Fielding writes: "[C]ompetition as a social ideal seems to me abhorrent; competition as a procedural device is morally repugnant because whatever other criteria one wishes to include or omit I would insist that part of one's characterisation contains some reference to working against others in a spirit of selfishness."[13] Simon states the criticism as follows: "The goal of competition is enhancement of the position of one competitor at the expense of others. Thus, *by its very nature*, competition is selfish. But since selfish concern for oneself at the expense of others is immoral, it follows that competition is immoral as well (italics added)."[14]

Critique of Positive and Negative Consequences of Competition

Advocates of the positive view of competition maintain that participation in competitive activities can help develop positive character traits and that these traits, such as courage, dedication, discipline, and perseverance, along with a competitive attitude, are necessary for surviving in our competitive world. Critics, on the other hand, suggest that negative consequences such as cheating, violence, and lack of learning opportunities, result from the "win at all costs" attitude which is promoted in competitive activities as a result of the negative consequences of losing. What are we to make of these supposed consequences resulting from participation in competitive activities?

First, a distinction must be made between causation and correlation. That is, if participants in competitive activities exhibit particular traits, be they negative or positive, it cannot be assumed that it was the competitive situation that caused these traits to develop. For example, people exhibiting dedication and perseverance would be the kind of people who would find competitive activity attractive. Jay Coakley illustrates this situation, and although he discusses physical traits, I would suggest that his argument is equally applicable to character traits.

> For example, if participants in youth sport programs were stronger, faster, and more coordinated than nonparticipants, would it be reasonable to conclude that strength, speed, and coordination among athletes were solely a result of their involvement in sport? Obviously, it would not. It is rather clear that children with certain physical attributes will be attracted to sport, and, once involved, they will be continually encouraged by peers, parents, and coaches. Furthermore, children who lack strength, speed, and coordination would be less likely to try out for competitive teams.[15]

Although Coakley is referring to youth sport programs where children and youth are free to participate or not, the argument would still hold for compulsory physical education programs; that is, children who develop positive characteristic traits may already have these traits prior to participating in physical education.

Thus, a distinction must be made between viewing participation in competitive activities as *causing* the development of "strong" personalities with the possibility that these personalities are the type who excel in competitive situations. Likewise, the negative consequences of cheating to ensure a win may not be caused by the competitive situation as much as by the ethics of the offending participant. Not all participants in competitive activities cheat, and those who do cheat might also exhibit such cheating behavior in other areas of their lives—for example, in academic tests, lying to parents, and so forth. Although such correlations are an empirical matter, it is important to point out that the claims made regarding the positive values and negative consequences of participation in competitive activities must not be considered as simply being *caused* by the act of competition.

The claim that participation in competitive activities is important as preparation for life must also undergo closer scrutiny. There are two points at issue here. Firstly, it may be questionable as to whether competitive attitudes *are* necessary for survival in our world and secondly, *if* this claim is accepted, *who* in fact is best prepared for life as a result of participation in competitive activities? The question regarding whether a competitive attitude is necessary for surviving in our world is, to a certain extent, an empirical question.

> For example, many managers have discovered that using competitive reward structures among employees often subverts the relationships the employees need to have with one another to perform their jobs efficiently. Success in today's world often depends much more on a person's ability to cooperate and to maintain intrinsic sources of motivation than on the ability to compete and the desire to dominate others. Those who are motivated only to outdo others often cut themselves off from the allies they need to become successful.[16]

Coakley cites examples of professionals such as doctors and lawyers forming organizations that restrict competition in their work lives, and leaders in the business world who, although proclaiming the merits of competition, get together to devise ways of concealing trusts, monopolies, and other anticompetitive practices so that they can increase profits while avoiding government sanctions. Thus, it is questionable whether a competitive attitude is as important as it is often claimed to be for surviving in our world. A point related to whether a competitive attitude is necessary for surviving in our world, concerns the desirability of a competitive world in the first place. As Charles Bailey notes:

> [T]he important point is that even if a given society can be shown to be highly competitive what can an educator deduce from this about what he ought to do and what he should teach? Surely it is still an open question whether children should be taught to "fit in" to the prevailing or majority ethos, or be taught to resist or at least be critical of such an ethos? The mere fact of a majority attitude accepting competition proves nothing.[17]

If, for the sake of argument, a competitive attitude *is* accepted as necessary for survival in our world (whether this *ought* to be the case will be left unexamined at present), the question arises as to who is best prepared for life as a result of participation in competitive activities. I suggest that those best prepared are those who frequently win. Fait and Billing would concur with this answer. "[C]ertainly there is value in experiencing both success and failure when striving for a goal, but it is extremely doubtful if those students with a steady diet of failure learn better how to compete; rather, they learn how to avoid failure through withdrawal, compensation, and rationalization."[18] Thus, one could argue that a consequence of participating in competitive activity is better preparation for life in a competitive world, but in this situation, a positive consequence for the winner is a negative consequence for the loser.

A discussion of winners and losers once again ushers in the issue of the inequality generated by competitive situations. Before accepting this inequality as a negative consequence of competition, a distinction must be made between *inequality* and *difference*. Ronald Dworkin makes a distinction between the right to equal treatment, "which is the right to an equal distribution of some opportunity of resource or burden," and the right to treatment as an equal, which is the right "to be treated with the same respect and concern as anyone else."[19] Dworkin cites the example of giving medicine to a child who is sick and one who is well. To treat the children as equal would require giving half of the medicine to one child and half to the other child. However, giving all of the medicine to the sick child would be compatible with equal respect and concern for both children. Thus, the children are treated differently but they are both being shown equal degrees of respect. Simon moves this distinction into the realm of competitive activities. "Accordingly, even though competition in sports may lead to unequal treatment, such as different assignments of playing time to better and worse players on a team or to a distinction between winners and losers of a contest, this is not sufficient to show that competition in sports is inequitable or unjust."[20] Likewise, in the realm of academics, it would not be considered unjust to award a high grade to an excellent paper and a lower grade to a poorer paper. What is critical to consider in this discussion of inequalities is the equal respect shown to participants in competitive activities.

Critique of the Intrinsically Positive and Negative Views

It is in examining the intrinsic value of competition where the positive and negative views of competition "collide head on." Those espousing a positive view of competition maintain that the very nature of competition involves striving together in the pursuit of excellence. Critics of competition maintain that competition is intrinsically selfish. In dealing with this dilemma, one must examine and evaluate counter-examples to each of these claims. It would seem quite simple to produce an example where the striving to pursue excellence in a competitive activity does not exhibit Hyland's conception of "competition as friendship."[21] The intentional harming of an opposing player in order to give one's team an advantage would be a good counter-example to the "competition as striving together" view. However, one must make a distinction here that parallels John Searle's distinction between "regulative" and "constitutive" rules. Some rules regulate antecedently existing activities, for example, "driving on the right-hand side of the road" regulates driving; but driving can exist prior to the existence of that rule. Other rules also create the very possibility of certain activities, for example, the rules of chess do not regulate "people pushing bits of wood around on boards in order to prevent them from bumping into each other," but rather "the rules are *constitutive* of chess in the sense that playing chess is constituted in part by acting in accord with the rules."[22] "Striving together" is constitutive of participating in a competitive activity and if regulative rules such as "not intentionally injuring an opponent" are broken, the potential "striving together" which constitutes competitive activity is not destroyed. Ideally, teachers (and society in general) should work against the breaking of regulative rules in order that what constitutes the competitive situation can flourish untarnished. In Arnold's words: "Whether or not this ideal is lived out as a part of a young person's upbringing is largely, if not entirely, a matter of how competitive sport is promoted and taught in schools. What then is being rejected, both on conceptual and historical grounds, is the view that competitive sport is inherently and therefore necessarily immoral."[23] Examples of "non-friendly" acts as they are currently practiced do not destroy the constitutive "striving together" involved in competition. To suggest that the breaking of regulative rules by some competitors destroys the possibility of "striving together" would be, in Francis Dunlop's words:

> [A]s unfair and inappropriate as judging philosophy from the betrayal of intellectual values that sometimes occurs among professional philosophers. Soccer violence and hooliganism is not a logical working out of the "essence" of a competitive game; rather as Bailey himself points out, a symptom of the general moral state of society.[24]

Critics of competition argue that competition lends itself to "violence and hooliganism" because of the selfish nature of competitive activities. To examine the claim that competition is intrinsically selfish requires an elucidation of the concept of "selfishness." As Simon points out, "if we define selfish behavior as self-interested behavior, then the pursuit of victory will be selfish, because we have stipulated it to be so by definition." He proceeds to cite two examples to which the concept of selfishness might be applied:

1. Jones is playing in a touch football game with friends. Jones says, "I'll be the quarterback." The others declare that they too want to be quarterbacks and suggest the position be shared. Jones replies, "It's my football! If you don't let me play quarterback, I'll take my ball and go home!"
2. Jones is in a spelling contest between two teams in her fifth grade class. She correctly spells a difficult word. As a result, her team wins and the other team loses.[25]

These examples would seem to be of two different kinds. As Simon points out, "[I]f there is an important difference between trying to defeat an opponent within a mutually acceptable framework of rules and simply disregarding the interests of others, then there is a significant, ethically relevant difference between athletic competition and selfishness."[26] Thus, the first example is a demonstration of selfishness since Jones is disregarding the interests of her teammates by demanding that she be allowed to be quarterback. In the second example, Jones is not disregarding the interests of her classmates when participating in the spelling contest. In fact, she is *respecting* the interests of her classmates by playing according to the rules, thus allowing the constitutive "striving together" of the competitive activity to occur in a *non-selfish* manner.

One further counter-example to the claim that competition is intrinsically selfish involves the necessity of opponents having to cooperate in order to participate in a competitive activity. Opponents must *cooperate* in their agreement to compete if competition is to occur. L. Perry notes that "competitions require us to assume the capacity to cooperate if they are to run at all."[27] Not only do opposing participants have to cooperate to "get a game off the ground," members of the same team in a team sport must cooperate if they are to be successful in playing the game. It would seem logically inconsistent that cooperative behavior is a necessary component of an activity which is intrinsically selfish.

Excellent Ends Justify Competitive Means

The intent of the preceding discussion was to demonstrate that "competition" should not be viewed as a contested concept. In critiquing the positive and negative consequences of participation in competitive situations, neither those propounding the positive nor the negative *consequences* of competition provide convincing arguments one way or the other.   However, when analyzing the views as to whether competition is *intrinsically* positive or negative, the former is a far more persuasive stance than the latter.

Regarding the positive and negative views concerning the *consequences* of participating in competitive situations, it does *not* appear that the arguments in favor of competition are more convincing than the arguments against competition or vice versa.   Recall the distinction made between causation and correlation as an attempt to dispel the claim that participation in competitive activities necessarily develops positive or negative traits in the participants.   By suggesting that only the winners really enjoyed the benefits of preparation for life in a competitive world (if it be the case that competitive attitudes are truly necessary or desirable for surviving in our world), it would appear that a positive consequence for the winner is a negative consequence for the loser in competitive situations.   By making a distinction between inequalities and differences, I suggested that participants may have different experiences, for example, one team wins and one team loses, but this does not have to imply that the losing team is treated with an unequal degree of respect, thus lessening the negative consequences for the losers in competitive situation.

Although in actual practice, participants do not always treat opponents or rules with respect, this situation does *not* negate the "striving together" that constitutes competitive activity.   Although critics of competition have suggested that competition is intrinsically selfish, a distinction can be made between disregarding the interests of an opponent on one hand, and on the other, trying to defeat an opponent within a mutually agreed upon framework of rules.   Agreeing to play within a framework of rules requires the cooperation of all participants. The necessity of cooperating in order to pursue a competitive activity is a persuasive counter-example to the argument that competition is intrinsically selfish.   The argument that competition is intrinsically positive, when conceived of as a "striving together," can withstand the counter-argument concerning the disrespect for rules and opponents which occurs because such an occurrence is not necessarily entailed by the competitive situation.   The "striving together" which constitutes participation in competitive activities is not negated by the disrespecting of regulative rules.   The onus is on teachers (and society) to work towards upholding respect for opponents and rules, and thus allowing the "striving together" involved in competitive activities to flourish untarnished.

To propose a persuasive argument in favour of competition requires not only an argument that competition is not intrinsically negative but also a demonstration that competitive situations provide an opportunity to grow, develop skills, and so on, which cannot be achieved without an element of competition. In order to demonstrate this, a revival of the root word *com-petitio* (to question together, to strive together) must take place. It is the notion of "together" wherein lies the opportunity provided by competitive activities for participants to grow and develop which cannot be experienced without an element of competition. It is only through comparison with something outside oneself that people are able to evaluate their skills and abilities and it is only through continued "striving together" with that "something" that people are able to realize their potential. This evaluating of skills and abilities through comparison with others would make it possible to meet Carr's third condition of exhibiting recognizable success at *x*ing.

The necessity of the "other" for realizing the potential for growth and development through competitive activity receives support from the work of social psychologists in the area of social comparison and social facilitation. Social comparison theory was originally formulated by Leon Festinger, who hypothesized that:

> (1) there exists, in the human organism, a drive to evaluate his opinions and his abilities . . . (2) to the extent that objective, non-social means are not available, people evaluate their opinions and abilities by comparison respectively with the opinions and abilities of others . . . [and] (3) the tendency to compare oneself with some other specific person decreases as the difference between his opinion or ability and one's own increases.[28]

The hypothesis that people prefer to compare themselves with others who have about the same ability level has found empirical support in other social psychological work.[29] This finding has important implications for physical educators in their deployment of competitive situations and these will be examined in the final section of this chapter. Social psychologists have attempted to explain this motivating influence of others performing the same task. Robert Zajonc hypothesized that the presence of others increases one's level of arousal. Robert Baron, Danny Moore, and Glenn Sanders further developed this theory and suggested that it is the conflict produced between the tendency to pay attention to the task being performed and the tendency to direct attention to the "other" which is arousing. Bradford Groff, Robert Baron, and D. L. Moore found that this conflict produces increased performance with simple tasks but decreased performance with more complex ones. This finding would have important implications for the timing of introducing competitive activities and these will also be discussed in the final section of this chapter.

Although social psychologists would propose that the social facilitation process requires comparison to actual people, it has been argued that the "other" with whom people "strive together" in *competitio* need not be limited to other people. Carolyn Thomas alludes to this situation in her discussion of the "other" as an essential element in competition.

> There is someone or something to go against or against which to measure success. Depending on the sport or the kind of competition, the "other" can be a person, self, a river or mountain, time, previous performances, or a score or person in abstentia such as in telegraphic meets. A related commonality is that an outcome is evident. There will be a winner(s) or loser(s), or you will either succeed or fail in the objectives that were established for the contest.[30]

The notion that a person can compete with a self, a river, or a previous performance has not escaped criticism. Peter McIntosh suggests that competing against oneself represents a conceptual impossibility. "I cannot both win and lose against myself, nor, when I improve my performance over last time, can I dissociate my present self from my previous self. Self-improvement is central to learning but it is not competition."[31] James Keating suggests that there are other, more accurate, ways to describe what a person is doing when he or she is referring to competing against him or herself. "He is attempting to improve his skill, to learn, to develop, to grow, to actualize his potentialities. Only when he seeks to exceed, surpass, or go beyond the best efforts of others is he actually competing. Competition in all of its forms always presupposes another or others."[32] Alice Kildea refers to competing against records as personal. "Attempting to beat the clock or to upend any record previously established by oneself (often referred to as the 'historic self') is an attempt toward excellence. It is personal rather than interpersonal activity. The pursuit of excellence is not competitive activity."[33]

Common to all of the above mentioned criticisms levied against the notion of competing against self, scores or records, is the distinction which is drawn between self-improvement and the pursuit of excellence on the one hand, and competitive activity on the other. However, the question must be raised concerning how a person knows if he or she has achieved excellence if not by comparison to others or to some standard. How can people speak of self-improvement if they do not have a standard by which to gauge progress? Thus, the very notion of excellence or improving oneself presupposes something by which people can compare their skills and abilities as well as the skill level they could potentially reach. This comparison requires competition because it is only in comparison to other people's skills and abilities (or records of skills and abilities set by other people) whereby a person can gauge his or her own abilities and the skill level he or she could potentially reach. The intimate connection between pursuing excellence and competition is evident in Simon's definition of competition as "a mutually acceptable *quest for excellence* through challenge (italics added)."[34] Paul Weiss, in describing "excellence," suggests that "[i]llustrating perfection, it [a superb performance] gives us a measure for whatever else we do." The connection between excellence and competition is evident in Weiss's words:

> The excellence that the athlete wants to attain is an excellence greater than that attained before. He wants to do better than he had; he would like to do better than anyone ever did. What he once achieved and what he might now achieve is an excellence relative to some particular period of time and circumstance. At another time and on another occasion, a superior state or performance will perhaps be produced, thereby making clear that man's final limits had not been reached before. This is a truth that will surely hold as long as men compete with one another.[35]

Concerning the people or objects against which one competes, a criticism can be levied against Thomas's conception of the "other" as including rivers and mountains. The critical distinction that must be made here involves the notion of intention.[36] A fellow competitor has the intention of striving together in a competitive activity. One's previous performance or score or record set by another person can still be perceived of as having at one time involved intention on the part of someone. A mountain or a river can never involve such intention. Thus, a person and a mountain or river do not strive together in the pursuit of excellence. A mountain climber or river rafter may achieve excellence but this is not determined by comparison with the mountain or the river but rather by comparison with the performance of another mountain climber or river rafter. The fact that mountains and rivers are graded does not negate my proposition that the comparison is between mountain climbers and river rafters since the mountains and rivers are graded on a scale which recommends that a climber or rafter be at a level comparable to an expert to tackle a mountain or river with a high grade, or that a climber or rafter need only be on par with a novice to attempt a climb or river run with a low grade.

When competition is viewed as a striving together in a pursuit of excellence, the "winning is everything" mentality dissipates somewhat. That is, people can still be developing in their pursuit of excellence even if they do not win a particular competition. As Weiss points out, "[E]ven the defeated gain from the game. They benefit from the mere fact that they have engaged in a contest, that they have encountered a display of great skill, that they have made the exhibition of that skill possible or desirable, that they have exerted themselves to the limit, and that they have made a game come to be."[37] Losing can also motivate players to improve their performance. Ross proposes that "a loss, much more than a win, goads coaches and athletes to improved performance."[38] Although competitors do not deliberately seek to lose (in an attempt to improve performance), teams will play superior teams, knowing the odds of losing are great. "Indeed, far from *avoiding* fixtures with teams to whom they are likely to lose, many clubs eagerly seek out such 'superior' opponents, since to play against a better side is usually more exciting and worthwhile, and tends to raise one's own game."[39] Thus, even though it is a logical necessity that the product of a competition is a winner (or perhaps a draw), it is obviously not the only reason people have for competing against others. As Arnold points out:

> *Trying to win* then may be considered a necessary feature of competing but this is not to be confused with a person's *reason* or *motive* for playing. For many school children (as well as for many adults) winning is a prospect rarely achieved but this does not prevent them wanting and continuing to compete and trying to win. Their reason for playing may be to do with fun, fitness, therapy, friendship, sociability, or the *pursuit of excellence* [emphasis added] rather than winning in order to "demonstrate their superiority over others."[40]

David Shields and Brenda Bredemeier reiterate the notion that to win is not the only reason for competing. "When the internal aim of competition–winning–is not the exclusive aim of the participant, competition can be a mutually enjoyable and satisfying means of *improving abilities*, challenging boundaries, and expressing one's affective need for exhilaration, joy, and community (italics added)."[41] If winning *was* the only reason people competed, they would deliberately seek out weak opponents to play against. However, spectators and players alike, enjoy the challenge of a "close" game. It is that "challenge" which epitomizes the striving together in pursuit of excellence which is made possible through competitive situations.

In summary, it might be helpful to look at the issue of competition in an ends/means light. That is, the gain of pursuing excellence with the heightened arousal attributed to the competitive situation justifies the means of participating in competitive activities which will sometimes result in losing. The gain of excellence is also worth the risk of a disregard for regulative rules, which arises as a result of living in a society that attaches such a negative stigma to losing. Although physical educators may not be able to change societal values regarding winning and losing, they can make progress in striving to defuse the "win at all costs" mentality by stressing the striving together in the pursuit of excellence.

Implications for Physical Education

Having explicated and critiqued conceptions of "competition" in their positive and negative forms, I concluded that the ends of pursuing excellence justified the means of competitive activity. However, a distinction was made between the "striving together" which constitutes competitive activity and the regulative rules that, if broken, do not negate the possibility of striving together in the pursuit of excellence. However, "striving together in pursuit of excellence" suffers abuse when competitors do not respect each other and the rules by which they have agreed to play. In order to avoid potentially disrespecting an opponent, some physical educators advocate competing against oneself or other standards as opposed to competing against other people. However, rather than avoiding competition with others because of the potential of disrespect for the opponent, physical educators must seriously strive to foster respect for opponents and rules. This topic will be examined in the following chapter.

Another attempt to avoid the potential abuses of competitive situations is evident when a distinction is made between "competitive sports" and "recreational sports." Parry refers to "*recreative sporting activities*, in which the participant engages primarily with a view to the pleasure, enjoyment, relaxation, entertainment, and so forth to be derived from them" and "*serious competitive sports*, in which the participant engages primarily with a view to winning and/or achieving high standards of performance."[42] However, making this distinction would seem to be in contradiction to a discussion of the nature of sport in an educational context. In Arnold's words:

> Without competition sport would not be what it is . . . . Sport, like mathematics or history, is what it is and is not to be confused with whether it is found to be recreative or can be taught in a recreative way. The educational justification for sport forming a part of the movement curriculum is that it is thought to be worthwhile in itself not because it may be found to have recreative value, even though this may be fortuitously the case. This point is not always understood by those who wish to transform the traditional view of sport, which is intrinsically competitive, into something else. If the teacher understands the nature of sport sufficiently well and is committed to it, the Lombardian ethic, where winning at all costs is emphasized to the detriment of social and moral values, will not be allowed to develop.[43]

Arnold is not suggesting that sport cannot be pursued for its recreational value. However, he is making a distinction between the *educational* value of sport lying in its competitive as opposed to its recreational nature. Key to the discussion regarding the nature of competitive sport is that the teacher understand competition to involve respect of opponents and rules. If this respect is fostered, competitive activities should not be discouraged in physical education contexts. However, respect for rules and opponents can only be fostered if teachers, through precept and example, help students see the value in respecting rules and opponents and the value in "striving together in the pursuit of excellence" made possible through competitive situations.

A criticism that is sure to arise and which must be addressed concerns the possibility of achieving competitive situations without the breaking of regulative rules in our present society. In a society which extols winners, it may not seem possible to engage in activities in which it is logically necessary to have a winner (or at least a draw) but in which winning is not necessarily the only important aspect of the activity. Since many students are unable to enjoy the valuable aspects of competition, that is, striving together to improve skill, grow, and actualize potential, because of the fear of losing, it is necessary to create situations where everyone has a chance at winning. An important factor in increasing the chances of everyone winning at some point relates to the social comparison theory discussed previously. As Edwin Delattre points out, "it is of the utmost importance for competitors to discover opponents whose preparation and skill are comparable to their own and who respect the game utterly."[44]

The importance of playing against students of comparable skill levels cannot be overemphasized. However, it would be an unusual physical education class where the students were all at the same level. Thus, it will be necessary to group teams with the same number of advanced and not as advanced students during team games. During individual activities, it is important that students are matched with someone of comparable ability. In the physical education setting, the teacher may have to be innovative in creating activities in which everyone at some point will win. For example, when playing baseball, the teacher should vary the pitcher so that the highly skilled pitchers are pitching to the highly skilled batters, while pitchers with slower pitches are pitching to the weaker batters.

Even when teams are paired up with evenly matched teams, members on the same team will not always have the same ability level. What often happens in games where not everyone can play at once is that the more skilled players monopolize playing time. Thus, a team may participate in a competition but not every member is able to "strive for excellence." In order that all students should receive the benefits of competing, the physical education teacher should avoid situations where students have to sit out. The teacher must ensure that all players have the opportunity to play. An example suggested by Thomas Tutko and William Bruns involved children's hockey teams in Chicago where a buzzer went off every two minutes and the coaches had to change their lineups. Another example which necessitates the involvement of more than a few players is a volleyball game where the ball has to be touched by three different players before it is passed over the net.

Not only must participants have the opportunity to play against competitors of similar ability levels and in the case of team sports, the opportunity to have their fair share of "playing time," another consequence of the preceding discussion concerns the timing of the introduction of competitive activities. Recall the claim made by social psychologists that social facilitation increases performance of simple tasks but decreases performance of more complex ones. This claim is substantiated by researchers in the area of physical education who propose a continuum of skill development. This continuum starts from a base of body management competence, moves into the development of fundamental skills and finally into the utilization of specialized skills.[45] It is only at the upper level of the continuum where students utilize their skills in a game setting. It is only after students have control of the necessary fundamental skills that the distraction of opponents is outweighed by the motivation these opponents provide. The upshot of this discussion then, is that once students have control over the skills needed for a particular activity, a competitive situation provides a heightened arousal which can result in improved performance, which captures the notion of "striving together in the pursuit of excellence."

Critics of competition raise questions such as "if the goal of competitive games is for students to compete and win, how can students accomplish either if they have not learned the prerequisite skills?"[46] I would counter that this situation does not require the removal of competitive experiences, but rather, it necessitates the teaching of the prerequisite skills. Children not only require the physical skills necessary for the competitive activity, but they must also be mentally and socially "ready."[47] The importance of social comparison cannot be overemphasized. As Glyn Roberts explains:

> Competition in sports is an evaluative system of normative social comparison in which being competent is important to children and to young boys in particular. Therefore, when we formalize the competitive experience as we do when we organize children's sports, we place the children in a very intensive evaluation process. For older children who are able to accurately attribute cause and effect relationships, this evaluation gives them important normative information relative to their own sport competence.[48]

The point that "competitive experiences give important normative information for children who are able to accurately attribute cause and effect relationships" must be reiterated. Thelma Horn is critical of competitive experiences because, in her words, "When we use competition, we are increasing this emphasis on peer comparison; they [students] then judge whether they are competent or not in an activity in terms of their peers. We are then strongly encouraging kids to look at their worth in terms of factors they have no control over (i.e., the skill of another child)."[49] However, if students experience progressive and age-appropriate tasks, they will learn to accurately attribute cause and effect relationships regarding their own skills and abilities and thus, the danger of attaching one's self-worth to another child's skill level, should be minimized.

In summary, if students are to enjoy the pursuit of excellence involved in participating in competitive activities, teachers must strive to create situations where opponents and rules are treated with respect. Teachers must also ensure that all students have the opportunity to compete against opponents of similar ability levels. Finally, the students must have a level of ability where they are in control over the necessary skills so that the addition of opponents will not undermine their ability to play. Thus, the onus is on the physical education teacher to create situations where everyone has a chance at winning. If students experience some wins, as well as losses, the hope is that they will enjoy the competitive activity for what it was meant to be—a striving together in the pursuit of excellence.

Chapter 5

The Necessary Role of Moral Education in Physical Education and Sport

The first four chapters have involved a justification for the inclusion of physical education in the educational curriculum based on the potential of acquiring practical knowledge through participation in physical activities. I based my argument, in part, on Carr's conditions for assessing practical knowledge situations. However, I could be criticized in that utilizing Carr's conditions for assessing practical knowledge as a basis for justifying practical knowledge could also justify learning how to engage in the "practical" activities of stealing or torturing.[1] To avoid this consequence, I propose that a fourth condition referring to moral acceptability be added to Carr's conditions for assessing practical knowledge. However, removing the possibility of unethical "practical knowledge" outcomes, we could still be left with the criticism that Carr's conditions for practical knowledge also justify the activity of "belly button scratching"[2] and the question can then be asked, "why should physical education activities be chosen over belly button scratching as a means to acquiring practical knowledge?" What distinguishes physical education activities from belly button scratching, or more typical "educational" practical activities such as the performing of science experiments or the solving of math problems, is the logical connection between moral education and physical education, as well as the possibility of the physical education class providing an arena for practicing moral behaviour.

In order to argue for a logical connection between physical education and moral education, I will have to explicate what I mean by both moral education and physical education. The literature concerning moral education is vast and the scope of this chapter precludes me from examining all of the issues involved in moral education. Thus, I will be making the following assumptions. I will assume that moral education is desirable and possible. I will also assume that there is enough agreement concerning what it means to be morally educated for us to examine how moral education relates to physical education.

When examining the relationship between moral education and physical education, I will have to make clear what is entailed in becoming physically educated. This will require an explication of the knowledge involved in physical education, an analysis of the role of competition in physical education, and finally an analysis of the nature of rules of games.

In suggesting that physical education provides an arena for the practicing of moral behaviour, I will have to deal with the counter-argument that sporting contexts have frequently been arenas for immoral rather than moral behaviour. I will also have to argue that the physical education class provides a context for the practicing of moral behaviour which is more conducive to this practice than the contexts provided by the math or science class. If physical education can be viewed as providing an important context for the practicing of moral behaviour, as well as being a subject that is intimately connected to the process of moral education, a strong justification will have been made for the inclusion of physical education in the educational curriculum.

Moral Education

Moral education is a topic that has received the attention of philosophers of education for millennia. Two of the main questions that have been addressed are: what constitutes "moral education," and how is this education best achieved. In examining "moral education," philosophers have made the distinction between moral "education" and moral "training." As Meakin points out:

> [I]mplicit in moral education, as I conceive of it, is the aim of fostering in pupils that degree of knowledge and understanding and that degree of emotional development which are necessary conditions of their coming to think critically for themselves on moral issues and of their making rational moral judgements which they translate into appropriate intentional action.[3]

In contrast to moral education, Meakin suggests that moral training suggests the "more limited aim of drilling pupils in a code of moral rules and concomitant behaviour patterns, with scant or no regard for their rationale . . . in the hope, or even expectation, that they will hold to them unshakably and live by them."[4]

As noted in the above quotations, implicit in the concept of moral education is the notion that moral rules and behaviour patterns can have a rationale; that is, there is some basis for making moral judgements. It is in seeking a basis for moral reasoning that many educators have turned to moral philosophy. Theories of moral philosophy can be divided into three categories: 1) deontological, 2) consequentialist, and 3) teleological.

The major type of deontological theory has been rationalism, and the classic example of such a rationalist theory is Kant's theory of the moral law which he called the categorical imperative. In the *Foundations of the Metaphysics of Morals*, Kant expressed the categorical imperative as follows: "Act only according to that maxim by which you can at the same time will that it should become a universal law."[5] Referring to such an imperative as "categorical," Kant is emphasizing that one has a duty to follow a particular maxim unconditionally, regardless of particular outcomes.

Where deontological theories are concerned with the "means" of moral decision making, consequentialist theories are more concerned with the "ends." The major type of consequentialist theory is utilitarianism. Utilitarianism is concerned with the consequences of particular actions. Specifically, utilitarianism is concerned with achieving the greatest good for the greatest number.

The major type of teleological theory would be that of virtue theory, first proposed by Aristotle but more recently having received renewed attention by Anscombe, MacIntyre, and Carr. Where deontological and consequentialist theories focus on *doing* (either based on duty or the consequences of an action), virtue theory focuses on *being*–being a certain type of person. "Human beings, like the members of all other species, have a specific nature: and that nature is such that they have certain aims and goals, such that they move by nature towards a specific *telos*. The good is defined in terms of their specific characteristics."[6] These specific characteristics are what educators would try to help their students develop in an effort to morally educate their students.

"How to" morally educate is the second major question addressed by philosophers of education. The approach one takes towards moral education will be based upon the moral theory (or combination of theories) one adheres to. The approach to moral education that may be considered "the dominant paradigm of research into questions of moral education and development in many leading contemporary academic centres for such enquiry"[7] is Lawrence Kohlberg's cognitive developmentalism. Nel Noddings highlights the connection between Kohlberg's theory and Kantianism: "Its [Kohlberg's theory] emphasis on moral reasoning, the primary place given to a single principle (Rawl's principle of justice), and its identification of 'moral' with the right rather than the good are all compatible with Kantianism."[8]

Kohlberg's theory has come under attack from a number of fronts. Perhaps the most publicized has been the debate between Kohlberg and Carol Gilligan. Gilligan proposed that because Kohlberg had developed his stages based on research he conducted with only male subjects, that the stages were biased towards males. A criticism that was levied earlier by Peters against Kohlberg's theory was that the theory neglected the moral significance of the acquisition of certain behavioural dispositions or character traits. Recently, Carr has brought the criticism concerning the neglect of character traits to the forefront in his development of an ethics of virtue theory of moral education.

Carr advocates a return to an Aristotelian ethics of virtue as a basis for moral education.

> [R]ather than evaluating moral judgements and responses in terms of their conformity or otherwise to certain rational canons of universal prescriptivity, one might seek to assess them in reference to their success in promoting the aims and purposes of a range of dispositions–the virtues–construed as constitutive of some ethically defensible conception of human well-being or flourishing.[9]

Carr's proposal that moral judgements can be assessed based on their success in promoting the aims of virtues construed as constitutive of an ethically defensible conception of human well-being has been criticized by A. Telling as not really finding the middle ground between Kantianism and utilitarianism which Carr thinks he has achieved.

> According to Carr, virtue theory shares with Kantianism the maintenance of certain moral values as being objectively good or bad ('lying is always bad', 'honesty is always good') but it differs from Kantianism in that these values are related to–or even derived from–some 'ethically defensible conception of human well-being or flourishing'. Virtue theory shares with Utilitarianism the idea that the consequences of acts (i.e., with respect to human flourishing) should be taken into account but it differs from

Utilitarianism in that acts which produce these consequences are viewed as internally related to human flourishing.[10]

Telling is critical of both Carr's concept of "ethically defensible conception of human well-being" and the distinction Carr attempts to draw between his theory and utilitarianism. Telling challenges Carr to explain "where an *ethically defensible* conception of human flourishing could be derived from if it is not from moral principles–which Carr seems to reject."[11]

Although Carr might be able to respond to Telling's challenge, I am not sure we have to jettison Kantianism in the way Carr wants to in order to have virtues play an important role in moral education. Jan Steutel, in an article entitled "The Virtue Approach to Moral Education: Some Conceptual Clarifications," provides three definitions of virtue approaches in an attempt to distinguish virtue approaches from other approaches, particularly Kohlberg's cognitive developmental approach. Under Steutel's first two definitions of virtue approaches, that is, traits of character as aims of moral education and traits of character are the only aims of moral education, Kohlberg's theory could still fall under Steutel's definitions.   Steutel points out that Kohlberg himself maintained "that a person who judges and acts in accordance with such a structure actually is the bearer of the virtue of justice."[12] Steutel suggests that the virtue of justice implies a number of other virtues, for example, "open-mindedness, tolerance towards rival conceptions and respect for rational arguments."[13] Although Steutel's third definition of virtue approaches, that is, moral education founded in an ethics of virtue, *does* exclude Kolhberg's theory because an ethics of virtue requires the primacy of aretaic terms (e.g., good, bad, virtuous, vicious) over deontic terms (e.g., right, wrong, duty, obligation), the aim of developing traits of character may be all we need to support a conception of moral education which involves both the acquisition of principles and the development of virtues.

Physical Education

The preceding discussion was intended to examine some of the issues involved in moral education. As mentioned in the beginning of this chapter, I was operating under the assumption that there was enough agreement concerning what it means to be morally educated that we could proceed to examine how moral education relates to physical education. People may adhere to different moral theories as their basis for making moral judgements, but I assumed that moral educators operated on the basis that moral judgements could be justified; thus, making moral education possible. Having examined a number of moral theories and resulting approaches to moral education, I concluded that one could hold a Kantian perspective but still advocate the aim of developing virtuous traits of character. I will now examine what it means to be physically educated, and in so doing, argue that there is a logical connection between moral education and physical education.

In chapter one I argued that physical education involves the teaching and (hopefully) the acquisition of practical knowledge, that is, "knowing how" to perform various movement skills, as well as theoretical knowledge, that is, knowledge of rules, strategy, and so forth, knowledge of how the body works, and knowledge of related fields such as exercise physiology, biomechanics, and so forth. I also argued that physical education programs provide an opportunity for social education, health education, environmental education, aesthetic education, and moral education. I now want to suggest that the relationship between physical education and moral education is more than just an opportunist one; rather, there is a logical connection between attaining knowledge in physical activities and the need for moral education.

The Role of Competition

To make the claim that there is a logical connection between moral education and physical education requires an analysis of the role of competition in acquiring practical knowledge. If we recall Carr's conditions for assessing practical knowledge, the third condition that one knew how to do *x*, was that he/she could exhibit recognizable success at *x*ing. How could one exhibit *recognizable* success if he/she did not have something or someone to compare him/herself to? As I argued in chapter four, competitive situations provide this potential for comparison of skills. In order to demonstrate this, a revival of the root word *com-petitio* (to question together, to strive together) is needed. It is the notion of "together" wherein lies the opportunity provided by competitive activities for participants to grow and develop which cannot be experienced without an element of competition. It is only through comparison with something outside oneself that people are able to evaluate their skills and abilities and it is only through continued "striving together" with that "something" that people are able to realize their potential.

A key point in my argument for the necessary role of competitive activities in physical education is the notion of competition as "striving together." This "striving together" necessitates a respect for one's opponents. All too often, competitors lose sight of striving together to improve their skills, and the desire to win results in disrespectful actions, for example, trash talk, intentional injuries, and so forth. Rather than avoiding competitive activities because of the potential for disrespecting opponents, the necessity for moral education becomes evident. As mentioned previously, moral education involves both moral reasoning and the development of virtuous traits of character. One of the most important ways a physical educator can help develop virtues such as benevolence, compassion, courteousness, fairness, self-control, and so forth, is to exhibit them him/herself. As Arnold points out: "He [the teacher] should understand that how to conduct oneself on the sports field is likely to be as much caught as taught. It is not enough then, that the teacher be a clear interpreter of the rules of sport. What is required in addition is to show himself as being genuinely committed to the forms of consideration and conduct it demands."[14] Teachers must take seriously their position as role models and diligently respect their opponents in the game.

Although "teaching through example" is an indispensable means of instilling respect in students, attention must also be given to the reasons participants give for respecting opponents, and this will require more direct teaching. "[T]o be fully moral one must do the right things as well as have the right reason. Both are required."[15] If the students are treating their fellow players with respect only because the teacher told them to, what will happen when the teacher is not looking? The physical education class provides ample opportunities for the teacher to stop a play and point out how a player is not receiving the respect that he or she deserves and seek reasons for why this situation occurred and why it creates a problem. Formal as well as informal discussion should be part of the teaching process. Meakin suggests that:

> [T]he aim would be to sensitize the developing child to the moral presuppositions of competitive sport and bring home to him that he has some degree of choice whether to abide (by them) or not. . . . The teacher should not only ask children whether they ought or want to behave in certain ways but, by an appeal to moral reasoning, should condemn "bad" practices and recommend "good" ones.[16]

Thus, through example and precept, teachers should do all that they can to instill the respect for opponents which allows the competitive "striving together in pursuit of excellence" to flourish.

Rules of the Game

As well as respecting opponents in the competitive activities which is an essential component of a physical education program aimed at teaching practical knowledge, students must also respect the rules of the game. The connection between rules and morality has received some attention in the philosophy of sport literature and it would be appropriate to examine the nature of these rules and how they relate both to moral education and physical education.

Some philosophers of sport and physical education have justified the moral education potential of physical education and sport by arguing that the necessity of following rules in order to play games requires a moral commitment. In Arnold's words: "Contestants agree that, both logically and morally, there is only one way to play the game fairly–and that is by the rules."[17] However, it could be argued that, although following rules may be logically necessary for playing games, it may not be a moral requirement. In fact, as Lesley Wright points out, the logical necessity of following rules works against the possibility that following these rules involves a moral decision. "For we recognize moral rules as such, first, because they belong to a particular moral system in which rational agents have a mutual interest, and secondly, because those who act according to the rules have some degree of choice. . . . But actions within the game carried out because of what the rules dictate are not freely chosen."[18]

Does this mean that following the rules of a game has nothing to do with the potential for moral education in physical education? I would answer that game rules do have a role to play concerning moral education, but this requires an examination of the nature of rules. One must make a distinction here that parallels Searle's distinction between "regulative" and "constitutive" rules. As mentioned in chapter four, some rules regulate antecedently existing activities, for example, "driving on the right-hand side of the road" regulates driving; but driving can exist prior to the existence of that rule. Other rules also create the very possibility of certain activities, for example, the rules of chess do not regulate "people pushing bits of wood around on boards in order to prevent them from bumping into each other," but rather "the rules are *constitutive* of chess in the sense that playing chess is constituted in part by acting in accord with the rules."[19]

This distinction between constitutive and regulative rules has been phrased in various ways by other philosophers as well as philosophers of sport. John Rawls distinguishes between rules of a practice and actions falling under such rules. "It is clear from what has been said that rules of practices are not guides to help one decide particular cases correctly as judged by some higher ethical principle. . . . To explain or to defend one's action, as a particular action, one fits it into the practice which defines it."[20] Thus, the rules of a practice are similar to constitutive rules, and keeping or breaking these rules are more of a logical than a moral matter.

Johan Steenbergen and Jan Tamboer utilize H. Lenk's distinction between "formal fair play" and "informal fair play," where formal fair play refers only to constitutive rules while informal fair play involves regulative rules. Steenbergen and Tamboer refer to philosophers[21] who regard the regulative rules as the only morally relevant aspect of sport.

> It is their opinion that the moral aspect of a rule-governed context arises not so much from the obedience to the constitutive rules, but rather from the attitude towards the rules and the opponent. This attitude transcends the 'playing according to the prescribed rules' attitude. Examples of informal fair play include: the idea of guaranteeing your opponent equal starting conditions and chances of winning, the esteem and respect with which the opponent is treated as playing partner or the participation of players of equal playing strength. Moral behaviour in sport, according to this point of view, cannot be derived from the formal rules.[22]

A final distinction that parallels the distinction between constitutive and regulative rules is the distinction between the actual rules and the "spirit" of the rules. Graham McFee uses the term "spoiling" in reference to breaking the "spirit of the rules," and he considers spoiling to involve a moral act. "I use the term 'spoiling' to roughly characterise approximately behaviour that, while not contrary to the rules of a game/sport, is nonetheless not how one *ought* to play it, for 'participating in the game/match' should mean participating in ways that respect one's opponents, showing due regard for them."[23] McFee gives an example of spoiling in cricket, but he is unsure how common other examples would be. I would argue that spoiling *does* occur

beyond the cricket pitch and Angela Lumpkin, Sharon Stoll, and
Jennifer Beller cite a fitting example concerning football:

> Paul Brown began his coaching career at Massillon High School in
> Massillon, Ohio. In 1928, his high school team was a little slow in the
> backfield. Brown analyzed the constitutive rules to find an advantage. He
> found one. The rules made no mention of what a uniform could or should
> look like, except that there must be a number on the back. Coach Brown
> seized the opportunity. He took footballs and cut them into two halves.
> He sewed one half on the front jersey of all the backfield players'
> uniforms. When the quarterback passed off, everyone appeared to have a
> football.[24]

Although some may consider Coach Brown's strategy to be a clever
one, I would (as would McFee) consider his action to be a good
example of spoiling.

McFee, in citing examples of cases that are *not* spoiling, makes it
clear that rules have to have been broken. But what if rules are broken
intentionally, with no attempt to deceive anyone, for example, the
intentional foul to change the momentum of the game? Should this
situation be considered breaking not only the "letter of the rules," but
something like the "spirit of the rules" as well? To make sense of this
situation, it would be appropriate to examine Fred d'Agostino's
discussion of the ethos of games. D'Agostino cites the example of
basketball, which is officially a "noncontact" sport. However, watching
any game of basketball, observers will witness countless incidents of
players making contact with each other, only a few of which will result
in the invocation of penalties. D'Agostino gives the following
explanation:

> This is so because the players and game officials have, in effect, conspired
> to ignore certain of the rules of basketball, at least in certain situations, in
> order to promote certain interests, which they share, for instance, with
> team owners and spectators–e.g., to make the game more exciting than it
> would be if the rules were more strictly enforced. . . . [Thus, there would
> appear to be] an unofficial *system* of conventions which determines how
> the official rules of the game will be applied in various concrete
> circumstances.[25]

In some basketball circumstances then, committing a foul may break a
formal rule but this act may still be acceptable according to the ethos of
the game. According to d'Agostino, the ethos of a game distinguishes

between behaviour that is permissible, behaviour that is impermissible (according to the rules) but acceptable, and behaviour that is unacceptable. The situation of impermissible behaviour that is acceptable makes for some tricky definitions regarding the morality of actions. As Robert Butcher and Angela Schneider point out: "The moral status of cheating flows from its definition. If cheating is all rule-breaking or even all intentional rule-breaking, then not all cheating is morally wrong. However, if cheating is breaking one's agreement, then all cheating is morally wrong, but not all rule-breaking is cheating."[26]

A potential way out of the impermissible but acceptable behaviour situation is to accept the suggestion that cheating involves breaking one's agreement. Thus, if teams agree to play by the ethos of the game, not strictly the rules, then breaking the rules that were still considered acceptable would be expected by both teams. Cheating would then occur only if one of the teams began breaking rules that fell outside the acceptable category. This situation brings us back to the Rawlsian distinction between practices and actions that fall under a particular practice. Thus, breaking rules that still fall within the ethos, or practice, of the game, can be justified by appeal to the practice. No independent moral justification is necessary. However, this situation is not immune to the question of whether the practice should be considered morally acceptable. This topic will be addressed in chapter six.

Physical Education as an Arena for Practicing Moral Behaviour

The preceding discussion regarding the nature of rules of games involved making a distinction between constitutive and regulative rules. Although deciding whether or not to follow constitutive rules may be more of a logical rather than a moral choice, students have a moral choice to make when it comes to following regulative rules as well as the "spirit of the rules." The option of following or not following regulative rules and the "spirit of the rules," as well as the necessity of respecting opponents when "striving together" during competitive situations, makes physical education an arena for the practicing of moral behaviour. Some philosophers have argued that the "arena" provided by physical education can become a context for immoral rather than moral behaviour. "[W]e can readily see that sports and games can and often are taught and learned in ways that conduce to the promotion of a wide range of morally suspect beliefs, dispositions and attitudes."[27] However, the key phrase here is that "sports and games can and often are taught and learned in ways that conduce to" immoral behaviour. Physical education teachers have a say in how sports and games are taught. By taking the logical connection between moral education and physical education seriously, physical education teachers can create "arenas" for the practicing of positive moral behaviour.

Although Carr argues that physical educators are in no way privileged over teachers of other subject areas regarding the opportunities for fostering positive moral behaviour, I would disagree. Firstly, regarding the importance of teaching students to respect others, physical education class would seem to provide more opportunity than a mathematics class for the degree of interaction between students. I am not suggesting that mathematics cannot involve students working together on solving problems, but mathematical problems can be solved by oneself. Games, dance, gymnastics, and outdoor pursuits, on the other hand, typically require more than one person to make the activity possible.

> By engaging in games, dance, gymnastics and outdoor pursuits children could learn through the guidance of the teacher, to become tolerant of one another, to be patient and to be co-operative. If the teacher was prepared to see his role as a moral educator, as well as a teacher of PE, then he could help to encourage attitudes of friendship and respect between members of the group and to discourage negative ones like meaness, hostility and spitefulness.[28]

Another reason I would propose regarding the unique situation of physical education for the development of moral education, has to do with the exemplification of moral concepts in a very literal way. As McFee points out, regarding moral notions in our lives: "[T]hose 'moral metaphors' are either *not* metaphorical or are *less* metaphorical in the sporting context, where there really can be fair playing and the levelness of actual playing fields. Seeing how these ideas interact with the rules (and spirit) of sport can show us how such notions might *apply*–and hence, perhaps, how they might be applied more generally."[29] Although a mathematics or science teacher should exhibit fairness in teaching, the physical education teacher cannot help but acknowledge the notion of fairness and level playing fields when it comes to placing students on teams (especially since the notion of "striving together" is best played out when teams have opposing teams which are well-matched). Thus, the physical education class provides a unique arena for the practicing of moral behaviour.

Chapter 6

Athletes, Ethical Issues and Moral Reasoning

The preceding chapters have all been philosophical in nature. Chapter five, in particular, involved an examination of moral philosophy. I concluded that participants in competitive activity must understand moral principles such as fairness and respect for others and then apply these principles to specific situations. Whether students/athletes do apply moral principles to specific situations is more of an empirical rather than philosophical question. Philosophers typically hypothesize examples that they then analyze. To analyze actual examples cited by athletes will be an important improvement in this process. To this end, I interviewed twelve university level athletes, asking the athletes to share examples of situations where they found themselves facing ethical issues. This line of questioning required the athletes to clarify their interpretation of an ethical issue. Having shared these issues, the athletes were then questioned as to how they came to some resolution.

The second phase of this project involved interpreting the athletes' answers concerning the reasons they gave for the decisions they made when resolving ethical issues. The framework I used in analyzing the words and experiences of the athletes was derived from moral philosophy. Most of the empirical research conducted in the area of sport and moral reasoning has focused on theories of moral development, for example, Piagetian or Kolbergian theories,[1] while most of the research concerned with moral theory/philosophy has been conceptual in nature.[2] This project was an attempt to integrate empirical research with a conceptual analysis derived from moral theory/philosophy.

The final section of this chapter examines the implications of the preceding analysis for moral education–specifically, the possibility of moral education in a physical education context.[3] An understanding of athletes' moral reasoning, or lack thereof, has significant implications for teachers and coaches who could be facilitating the development of the critical thinking skills and dispositions required in moral reasoning. The connection between critical thinking and moral reasoning is important. As Siegel notes:

> [A] morally mature person must recognize the centrality and force of moral reasons in moral deliberation, and moral education must seek to foster that recognition. Such "rational virtues" as impartiality of judgment and recognition of the force of reasons, to name just two such virtues, are indispensable to moral education. They are also, we have seen, central aspects of critical thinking.[4]

I will argue that physical education programs provide an opportune context for developing moral reasoning skills and dispositions in both students who will continue on in sports as well as those who will not become elite athletes.

What Athletes Have to Say

I randomly chose twelve athletes, attempting to achieve a gender balance. However, because there were fewer women's teams than men's teams, eight of the athletes interviewed were men and four were women. I also attempted to achieve representation from the variety of sports teams involved in the university athletic program. This process resulted in interviews with five individual sport athletes and seven team sport athletes.

Over half of the athletes interviewed had difficulty defining an "ethical issue." They usually ended up citing examples, such as cheating, playing dirty, trash talking, and taking drugs. Those athletes who were able to articulate some sort of definition related ethical issues to the obedience to or the breaking of rules, for example, "A situation in which you have to weigh whether you go against what the rule is or go with the rule, because the choice is either winning or losing." Other athletes gave broader definitions, concerned mainly with doing what was right or wrong, for example, "Deciding whether it's right or wrong and what consequences you'll have to face," "You're faced with sort of the right and wrong, the ways that you should conduct yourself, sort of the standards," "Maybe what's acceptable or what's not acceptable." One athlete brought in the notion of guilt, as well as not harming people: "Doing things that I'm not going to feel guilty about afterwards would be being ethical. And doing things that aren't going to harm people."

A few athletes' answers were concerned not with harming people, but rather harming the nature of sport, for example, "People–administrative people, coaches, doing things that isn't [sic] in the nature or spirit of sport. That would be unethical, in my opinion," "Ethics is more like . . . more of your attitude I guess, towards a sport. This is the way I think of ethics and stuff, like the way you work, things you do to get yourself ready for games and practicing situations and stuff like that," "Something that will bring up a lot of stink in the whole . . . in the whole area of sport, just anything like judges, officials, disqualifications, coaching types, coaching." An interesting perspective concerning the "nature of the sport" was raised by the answers given by the hockey players. It was interesting to note that the two hockey players interviewed did not consider the fighting involved in hockey to be regarded as "dirty play:" "I mean, that's the way the game's played by nature. I mean, as a fan going to a game you want to see a good physical game where there's a lot of hard hitting," "I can try and get other players off their game on the other team by giving them a little shot and stuff like that and a couple cheap shots, but that . . . I mean that's coming back to it again, we consider that part of the game." One of the hockey players made fighting for a team sound almost ethical: "Yeah, probably when you're fighting for your team it is more ethical, or noble than when you're just fighting for yourself." It was interesting to note that the hockey players could not think of any ethical issues in their sport.

The ethical issues shared by the athletes could be grouped into those that could harm other people and those that could harm the nature of the sport. A further categorization could be made between those issues which involve preparation for the game, for example, taking drugs, and those that occur during the game, for example, playing dirty and trash talking. It should be noted that issues that occur pre-game and during game could hurt both people and the nature of the sport.

Having shared examples of ethical issues in their respective sports, the athletes were asked how they would resolve these issues. The answers given by the athletes were surprising but encouraging. Either university level athletes are unique as an athletic level, or I randomly chose very ethical athletes, or athletes are hesitant to share unethical behaviour; but all ten athletes who were able to come up with examples of ethical issue, leaned toward what most people would consider the more "positive" choice, for example, not taking drugs, not fighting, and so forth. The possibility that athletes might not represent their ways of dealing with ethical issues honestly did not really matter for the purposes of this study. What *did* matter was the *reasons* the athletes gave for making their decisions. The reasons the athletes gave could be divided into six categories: reasons concerned with 1) "doing unto others as you would have them do unto you," 2) fairness, 3) respecting others, 4) not hurting the team, 5) respect for the game, and 6) fear of getting caught. What should be noted is that these categories are not exclusive. In fact, the first three categories are very inter-related. The inter-relatedness of these categories will become evident in the "Interpretation" section.

Four of the athletes' reasons fell under the "do unto others as you would have them do unto you" category. When one of the athletes was asked if he would "fudge" his weigh-in, he responded:

> Well, that would raise a lot of concerns with me simply because by me accepting that I would fear that everyone else was doing it. When you have an honour system, it's there for a reason and that's to keep a certain balance . . . to keep some fairness and incompromise and integrity in any situation. You take that away on one part, yeah, you might be burning someone else but then you can be burned back. And that's just a situation I wouldn't want to be involved in. I'd rather keep things on an even playing field.

This same athlete experienced some tension with the "do unto others" attitude:

> In the middle of a match, to be frank with you, I've attacked knees. I mean, I've got a bad knee right now. I wouldn't want it done to me at this point in the game, but it. . . . There is . . . I guess there's a line and I guess it's there . . . I shouldn't say there's a line. There probably is a grey area and the way we perceive it really tends to be in the different situation.

When another athlete was asked why he would not "play dirty," his response was "I don't know. I've just, I've always hated when people played dirty on me." The track athlete, when asked why he would not cut another runner off, responded: "I don't want to interfere with them because you don't want it to happen to yourself as well." "Doing unto others" can also apply to your own teammates. One athlete, in reference to backing up a teammate, stated that:

> the thing is that if I didn't back him up, the next time maybe the situation might be in my hands or I might not be able to handle someone and I might not . . . and he might not even come and back me up just because the fact that I didn't do it for him before.

The second category of reasons had to do with the issue of fairness. Two athletes made explicit reference to the notion of "fairness". The athlete quoted above regarding the "weigh-in" system, stated: "When you have an honour system, it's there for a reason and that's to keep a certain balance . . . to keep some *fairness*. . . . I'd rather keep things on an even playing field, you know (italics added)." The sentiment of an "even playing field" was raised by another athlete: "You know that in a race everything's supposed to be fair to each . . . each athlete, so . . . all the conditions are supposed to be fair, so you don't wanna . . . you know, I guess win on the . . . not the same terms as everybody else."

Related to the issue of fairness is the third category of reasons given concerning the resolution of an ethical dilemma; that being a respect for others. The athlete who did not want to cut another runner off, did not want that to happen to him, but he also pointed out that by cutting others off "you're disrespecting other runners." The athlete who would back up his teammate (for the reason that he would want to be backed up as well), also stated that "I mean you just kind of do it out of . . . out of respect for the person and just 'cause he's your teammate and you don't want him getting hurt or . . . or anything."

Closely related to "respecting your teammates" (not necessarily your opponents) is the fourth reason, not hurting your team. As one athlete put it: "You don't do chopping in practice, cause your own teammates. You don't want to hurt your own friends, your own team." Besides not physically hurting their own teammates, some of the athletes wanted to make sure their teammates were not hurt by the opposing team:

> But we've had circumstances this year where we've sent guys off the bench to go out and fight other players on other teams just to kinda get a message across. So that may be . . . I mean, for me that's not really unethical. That's part of the game if the team's going after your best player, I mean, you have to do something to stop that. But for a person like yourself or a fan, you may think "well, he's sending him out to beat

someone up! That can't be ethical." But from the player's perspective, I mean, you see that as part of the game. You don't want your best players getting injured and you have to take measures to stop that.

Protecting one's teammates need not only apply to physical protection. Some players felt that they had to protect their teammates verbally by returning trash talk being directed at a teammate.

> If someone's . . . you know, going to do something to your teammate. You want to be there right behind him and back him up or something. You know, if someone's going to trash talk you, then you [sic] just gonna let it . . . the same guy that's trash talking your teammate, you better tell him the same thing or give him something back.

This same athlete used an interesting military analogy: "So, it's pretty hard to win when you don't have six guys that are going to be right behind each other like, if you're going to go to war with each other on the court, you gotta have six guys that are going to go to war with each other." Another athlete shared a similar military example: "It's a team sport so if I do something that causes a penalty, my team suffers. It's like in the military. You know, one person does it and the whole platoon has to do push ups or whatever. So it's . . . it has to do with whether you're a team player or an individual, I think." Concern for the team is evident in the example of an athlete choosing to avoid a penalty: "Sometimes you think, 'oh, I just wanna slash him,' but then I think, 'well, then I might get a penalty and that might put my team down even worse'," "I mean, there's times I just lose it and I just go but most times I think you think, okay, well I mean I can't do this because it's gonna hurt my team in the long run," "I'm a team player. I'm more concerned with my team than just me. So, I mean if somebody's giving me a cheap shot, I'll be mad, but you know I try not to do anything that'll harm my team."

The fifth reason some of the athletes gave for making the decisions they made concerning ethical dilemmas had to do with a respect, not so much for others, but for the game and one's ability to play the game. The notion of respecting the game was made clear in an eloquent response by one of the wrestlers:

> It feels good to fully understand something. Like, to fully understand the sport of wrestling and like, there's all the physiological things going on, there's all the physics, the energy system parts of it. There's just a

plethora of angles and everything . . . like, there's math galore going on. . . . There's everything going on in this five minute span and, God, I just want to be able to experience them all.

This same athlete was more concerned with improving his wrestling skills than winning. In reference to his coaches' words: "We'll pick things that we want you to practice and be well at, and focus on those things. And that made me get away from wanting to win." The desire to improve skills as opposed to winning was not always this athlete's goal. In reference to when he was younger: "Winning means peers, so you wanna win." Another athlete was also not that concerned with winning, and her reasons included the enjoyment of the sport itself as well as extrinsic reasons:

Like, I don't have the big goals to win an Olympic gold medal, like, I'm more of a swimmer to swim because I enjoy it and because it has health benefits for me, it's . . . I have fun, and meet friends, and stuff like that and, you know, it's not that big of a deal for me not to come home with a huge medal all the time.

Respecting the game seemed to imply respecting one's ability to play the game, that is, one's skill. In giving reasons for why she would not "trash talk," one athlete said: "I wanna be, you know respected and for what I can do, and not for what I . . . how I behave like an idiot, in my opinion." This same athlete emphasized the importance of skills: "You know, I don't wanna win that way. If I'm gonna win, I'm gonna win because of how I execute my skills and that . . . and not that I'm trying in someone's head, you know." Related to the use of skill, was the notion of playing the game "on your own" as opposed to cheating (through the use of drugs, rule-breaking, and so forth). "I don't think you get the same satisfaction out of it if you don't do it on your own" or "For me, personally, there would be no satisfaction in winning something that I cheated for." The athlete who saw no satisfaction in cheating to win summed it up: "Like, just play the game, and that sort of thing . . . and I don't get the rest of it . . . in my head, it doesn't make sense." Another athlete reiterated this sentiment: "You know, I just wanna play the game."

The sixth reason, fear of getting caught, was only expressed by one athlete, and this athlete, upon further reflection, decided she would not cheat. Regarding her refusal to use performance-enhancing drugs, this athlete responded: "But you never know, 'cause I don't know if I'm doing it because it's so much . . . right to do. Maybe I'm doing it because they can test me at any time and I don't want to be caught." It is interesting to share in this athlete's moral reasoning process regarding her refusal to use drugs:

> Why do I do it? I suppose the biggest reason is being caught. But . . . I don't . . . I suppose there's always ways you could get around it if you really had to so I suppose I'm not doing it because it's wrong. But . . . I guess it's hard until you've really been pressured to do it and someone's. . . . So, if someone comes up to you and says, "there's absolutely no way you're going to be caught," how are you going to do it? But I don't think I would. But I suppose you really don't know until you get that chance. But I don't think I would. No. No. I think I want to achieve it on my own.

Although this athlete is sharing her moral reasoning process, some athletes said it was not possible to reason this way while playing the game:

> Especially at our level, it's very fast and very high level. It's your thinking. I find when I'm thinking out on the ice, that's when I get into trouble because . . . well, I'm a lot slower. I have to go on my instincts and reactions so it's just the way it goes. . . . Like you do the thinking ahead of time and then when you get into the game, it's all reaction. And when you're going on reaction, sometimes anything can happen, like that's when your emotion may take over so you have to try and keep things in equal balance.

When asked whether the "pre-game thinking" involved thoughts on ethical dilemmas, the athlete responded: "No, it's mostly just like . . . breakout, forechecks, and stuff like that. . . . I've never thought of the ethical aspects of a . . . of the game." Whether athletes should be thinking of the ethical aspects of the game will be examined in the final section of this chapter.

An Interpretation of the Athletes' Reasons within the Framework of Moral Philosophy

Moral philosophy is a well-established scholarly discipline, but the application of insights gleaned from a study of this discipline to the practice of sport has not received much attention in the scholarly literature. In chapter five, I summarized, albeit briefly, theories of moral philosophy. Theories of moral philosophy have traditionally been divided into three categories: 1) deontological, for example, Kantism, 2) teleological, for example, virtue theory, and 3) consequential, for example, ethical egoism.[5] The resolution of a moral issue can be interpreted from one or the others of these three perspectives.

In reviewing the reasons the athletes gave, I was able to distinguish six categories of reasons–reasons concerned with 1) "doing unto others as you would have them do unto you," 2) fairness, 3) respecting others, 4) not hurting the team, 5) respect for the game, and 6) fear of getting caught. In analyzing these categories, it becomes evident that all three types of moral theory come into play. The first category "doing unto others as you would have them do unto you" is a prime example of Kant's categorical imperative: "Act only according to that maxim by which you can at the same time will that it should become a universal law."[6] The second category concerning fairness is intimately related to Kant's categorical imperative. If some behaviour would cause an element of "unfairness," then the whole construct of the game or contest is in jeopardy. As Sheila Wigmore and Cei Tuxill point out: "To will that everyone in a game should cheat would be to render cheating impossible, as well as pointless, since cheating or unfair play is only a meaningful activity if everyone else involved is playing fair, and it is assumed that they are doing so."[7]

The third category involving respect for others is a prime example of Kant's second form of the categorical imperative: "Act so that you treat humanity, whether in your own person or in that of another, always as an end and never as a means only."[8] An example of treating a person as a means, rather than as an end, would occur if an athlete decided to cheat because he or she would be using his or her opponents only as a "means" to win the game. Once more, Wigmore and Tuxill note the importance of this Kantian principle:

> Cheating, from this perspective, also involves a cognate "means-end" reversal, that constitutes a failure of respect for persons, since other players become merely means to the ends of the cheat, rather than equal participants in a joint and conscious purpose and activity; they are used as a means to an end which is not theirs and to which they have not consented.[9]

It is important to point out, when following the Kantian duty of respect for persons, that "persons" would include not only your own teammates, but also your opposition. Arnold relates the notion of Kantian respect to altruistic behaviour:

> Altruism is perhaps best understood as having to do with those forms of action and conduct that are not done merely because of what is fair and just in terms of playing and keeping to the rules but because, in addition, there is a genuine concern for, an interest in, and concern for one's fellow competitors, whether on the same side *or in opposition* (italics added).[10]

The fourth category of "not hurting the team" may on the surface be perceived as an example of a Kantian respect for persons. However, a distinction seemed to be made here between one's own team and the opposition; that is, the athlete would be concerned about not hurting one's own team, but hurting the opposition was not an issue. Thus, this reason is less of a respect for persons and more of an exhibition of the virtue of loyalty; thus we have an example of virtue theory in action.

The teleological theory proposed by Aristotle could also be seen as applying to the fifth reason concerned with respect for the game. Although virtue theory would seem to apply only to humans, Aristotle applied his conception of *telos*, or inherent nature, to all things, human or not.[11] If we consider respect for the game to involve respect for the inherent nature of the game, athletes who chose to focus on improvement of skills rather than solely on winning the game would appear to be seeking the inherent nature of competitive games (recall the latin root word of *com-petitio* meaning "striving together").

The sixth reason cited in resolving ethical dilemmas involved the fear of getting caught. This reason would be an example of the third type of moral theory, the consequentialist theory, particularly ethical egoism. The ethical egoist would always do what would promote his or her greatest good and would refrain from doing what would not promote his or her greatest good. In most cases, "getting caught" would be an example of something which would not promote one's greatest good, thus an ethical egoist would refrain from making a choice which could result in the possibility of getting caught. Having analyzed the words and experiences of the athletes interviewed, within the framework of moral theory, we turn now to a discussion of the implications of this analysis for the possibility of moral education in a physical education context.

Implications for Moral Education

The preceding discussion has important implications for the possibility of moral education in a physical education context in at least three ways. First of all, the responses of the hockey players interviewed open up the whole area of whether sport experiences should be subjected to the same moral considerations as other life experiences. That is, for example, should considerations of respect and fairness apply to sports as they do to other human activities? If an affirmative answer is arrived at, then the possibility of providing an education in the area of moral reasoning becomes tenable. This possibility leads to the second area where the interviews with the athletes can be informative; that is, reviewing the categories of reasons cited and their reflection of moral theory can help teachers and coaches facilitate the development of moral reasoning skills in their students and athletes. Finally, the very possibility of the athletes articulating the reasons they have for making certain ethical decisions has implications for how teachers and coaches can help facilitate the development of moral reasoning. I will consider each of these areas in turn.

The hockey players interviewed were unable to think of any ethical issues in their sport. It was not the case that they were denying that their hockey games involved fighting, cheap shots, infractions of rules, and so forth, but that these behaviours were justified because "that's the way the game's played by nature." This sentiment raises the fundamental issue of whether sport experiences should be subject to the same moral considerations involved in other life experiences; that is, does the "nature of the game" permit behaviour which could be deemed morally unacceptable outside the context of the game? The paradigm example of this situation would have to be boxing. If the possibility of fighting was removed from hockey, we could still have a hockey game–this would not be the case with boxing. "[B]oxing looks morally incongruous with the rest of life. Those responses to other selves, which outside the ring would be unacceptable and mystifying, are appropriate and lauded inside the boxing ring. No explanation is required for that vicious ferocity inside the ring towards another self."[12] Perhaps it is time that a civilized society seeks an "explanation" for this sort of activity. The explanation alluded to by the athletes interviewed concerned the "nature of the game." It is true that games are social constructions, involving self-contained means and ends. But does this imply that larger issues such as issues of morality should have no impact on such self-contained activity? Gordon Reddiford, in an article entitled "Morality and the Games Player," has one of his proponents make a distinction between moral rules, one of whose characteristics is the possibility of universalizability, and constitutive rules made by groups or individuals which make certain practices possible, for example, rules of games, parliamentary procedure and wedding ceremonies. Unlike moral rules, these constitutive rules are not universal. However, Reddiford points out:

> It does not follow from this distinction that there are some areas of life that are pre-eminently moral and some that are only, so to speak, derivatively so–that there is an inside/outside distinction to be made in moral matters. It is not the case that those engaged in rule-governed practices of the sorts indicated only partake of morality in some secondary sense, that when, for example, they wish to justify what they do when playing a game the players must have resort to some purer, primary, moral sphere.[13]

Reddiford supports this contention by making a further distinction between the *formal* rules of a game, for example, what counts as offside, and the instrumental activities, for example, strategy, which are not the subject of legislation. "Since games permit a wide range of instrumental actions they leave open the possibilities of acting morally or immorally."[14]

Another way of looking at the moral culpability involved in human-constructed practices, is to view the possible behaviours within the practice as existing along a continuum. A paradigm case here would be that of war (an analogy to sport which was actually cited by some of the athletes interviewed). The "rules" involved in the practice of war differ from the rules involved in a non-war situation, for example, it is acceptable to kill your enemy in war time whereas it is not acceptable to kill during peace time. However, there are still rules regarding war-time killing, for example, limits on chemicals in warfare. Returning to the boxing situation, Paul Davis questions the culpability of boxing:

> If boxing does not essentially promote violence [he supports this argument by emphasizing the disciplined and regulated nature of boxing], it is questionable whether boxing should be placed in the dock, in the case where contingent features of context allow it to play a causal role in the generation of some violence. We do not believe that beer producers are a priori implicated in alcoholism, nor car manufacturers in road fatalities, nor candy makers in premature tooth decay.[15]

Returning to the concept of the continuum of moral behaviour, we can see that beer producers can encourage vast amount of alcoholic consumption, or they can remain silent on drinking habits, or they can promote responsible drinking (as do many beer companies in their campaigns against drinking and driving). Likewise, car manufacturers can emphasize the high speeds that their cars can reach, or they can remain silent on road safety, or they can promote responsible driving (as witnessed in the "speed kills" campaigns evident in Manitoba, Canada). The analogy with boxing could suggest the possibility of "giving and parrying of light blows with no intention of striking the opponent severely,"[16] or something similar to what we see in Olympic style boxing, or what we witness in professional boxing. Anywhere along this continuum, we might say that a "morality line" has been crossed.

Whether we argue for the applicability of moral rules to sport based upon the possibility of behaving morally or immorally during instrumental activities (as opposed to simply breaking or adhering to formal rules), or whether we take the line of argument that sport activities involve behaviours which fall along a "moral continuum" and at some point, a behaviour has "gone too far," athletes will encounter moments when a decision has to be made concerning whether a particular behaviour would violate a moral rule or push an issue of morality "too far." In order for athletes to make such decisions, they must have some underlying moral theory to guide them. The responses provided by the athletes interviewed showed that this was the case. The analysis of the words and experiences of the athletes demonstrated that the reasons they gave when resolving ethical issues could be interpreted as being based upon all three major types of moral theory, that is, deontological, teleological, and consequentialist theories. However, it appeared that most athletes' reasons fell under only one of each of these moral theory categories. This provides important information for the teacher or coach interested in facilitating the development of his or her students'/athletes' moral reasoning skills and dispositions.

If athletes (or anyone, for that matter) consider only one moral perspective when deliberating over an ethical issue, important considerations may be overlooked. Thus, it is important to have a grasp on more than one moral theory in order to give an ethical issue the most comprehensive consideration possible. As Arnold points out:

It will be seen that the Kantian view of morality has a lot in common with the justice theory of sport as well as with those preconditional features of sportsmanship which are to do with fairness. In stressing the universal and impartial, however, the Kantian view seems to overlook or disregard some aspects of interpersonal relations which are as morally important in sport as in other spheres of life. I refer to such virtues as sympathy, compassion, concern and friendship.[17]

Thus, Arnold is arguing for a consideration of Kant's deontological theory as well as a version of virtue theory. Zeigler argues for what he calls a "triple-play approach," where someone contemplating an ethical dilemma would follow three steps: 1) Kant's Test of Consistency, 2) Mill's Test of Consequences, and 3) Aristotle's Test of Intentions.[18] There will, of course, be moments where considering various moral theories will result in conflicting prescriptions. However, this does not mean that teachers and coaches should avoid teaching various moral perspectives–rather, the importance of facilitating critical thinking skills in their students and athletes becomes apparent.

The greater the ability to reason, the better able we will be to address moral issues. Moral reasoning is a problem-solving activity, a way of trying to find answers. It is no different than any other logical and systematic process except that it involves offering reasons for or against moral beliefs. Moral reasoning is a way to critique questions and answers. It is not limited to a defensive position of what we believe or know to be right, rather, our purpose in moral reasoning is to discover the truth. In moral reasoning, opposing positions are analyzed to decide whether we should agree or not.[19]

The ability of the interviewed athletes to articulate reasons for choosing one or another action in an ethical issue demonstrated not only which moral theory their reasons were based upon, but also the importance of discussion concerning ethical issues. This has important implications for the coach or teacher in a physical education context. As mentioned in chapter five, one important means by which a coach or a teacher can facilitate moral development is through example. Although "teaching through example" is an indispensable means of instilling moral values, attention must also be given to the reasons participants give for behaving morally, and this will require more direct teaching. Thus, through example and precept, teachers should do all that they can to help facilitate the moral reasoning skills of their students and athletes so that participation in sports can be seen as an opportunity to practice moral behaviour rather than as an occasion to practice immoral behaviour, which not only impedes the participants' own moral growth but also tarnishes the possibilities inherent in sport to provide a practice field for morally appropriate behaviour.

Chapter 7

Coaches, Ethical Issues and Autonomy

For the previous chapter I interviewed university-level athletes in an attempt to ascertain what sort of ethical issues these athletes encountered in their sport and how they resolved these issues. A topic that arose in the interviews concerned the influence of the coach on the athletes' perception and resolution of ethical issues in their sport. To better understand the influence of the coach, I conducted a subsequent study where I interviewed university-level coaches. I asked the coaches questions similar to those asked of the athletes–questions pertaining to examples of ethical issues and how the coaches resolved these. A further question asked of the coaches concerned the notion of autonomy–how much autonomy should athletes be given in resolving ethical dilemmas in their sport.

In this chapter I will examine the ethical issues shared by the coaches, including how the coaches resolved these issues. I then compare and contrast the coaches' perceptions and resolutions of ethical issues with the answers given by the athletes. Differences between the coaches' and athletes' perceptions and resolutions of ethical issues raises questions concerning the autonomy of the athlete. Thus, I conduct a conceptual analysis of the notion of autonomy. I consider different conceptions of autonomy and how each conception translates into the coach-athlete relationship.

Ethical Issues Faced by Coaches

Before sharing examples of ethical issues faced by the coaches and their athletes, the coaches were asked to define an ethical issue. The most common theme to emerge from their answers had to do with making a decision between doing something which would be better for the team, that is, a win, or doing something which would be better for the individuals involved–including the coach, who's moral principles might be compromised if the first action was chosen.

I would define an ethical issue as a situation where a coach has to make a decision philosophically whether to go ahead with something where in one case it may be better for the team, but in the case of humanistic development or his philosophy in life probably goes counter to what is the norm.

I feel an ethical issue is something that I know that there is kind of two sides to it whereby if you go one route, you know that probably you are doing the right thing, but the other side of that which creates the dilemma is that if you do the so called "right thing," you may not get the maybe immediate results that you need to get, and to me that is where the dilemma comes in. You know you are giving something up to either do something that is right by the team, player, colleague, just pure morals and ethics, you know and you may lose out on something. You may lose out on something like winning.

An issue . . . I would think . . . if you do something and the end result usually it's about winning or losing . . . in effect then you may be challenged as to what your . . . ethically, you may think the right choice is A, but the outcome of that choice is not what you want.

The coaches' perception of an ethical issue as a choice between what would be best for the team, that is, a win, and what would be best for an individual, played itself out in the examples of ethical issues shared by the coaches. One of the most recurring examples of an ethical issue shared by the coaches was whether to play an injured athlete.

I guess one common one [issue] would be a player's ability to play if injured and whether . . . you always have that issue of . . . of whether they're actually ready to play or not and it would certainly be an asset to the team if they'd play, even if they'd only play sixty or sixty-five percent of their capability, they'd still be an asset to the team. But it's at . . . at the risk . . . at the risk of the person's, I guess, well-being or . . . their health.

I look on it as some sort of a struggle between, should I really play this player because it is not right for her, should I play this player because I need her to play.

I think of the injury situation, whereby you know a player is injured and you try to rationalize and define the injury by "okay Joe, are you injured or are you hurt?" Well, really they are the same thing. But I know I've done it and I know a lot of coaches who use that definition in terms of injury.

The other frequently recurring example shared by the coaches concerned whether to play a player who had missed practice.

You have rules for teams. These rules should be consistent with all players in the program. Now, player A misses or is late for two practices and you are in a big game on the weekend and that player has a big impact. Ethically, you should not start him and should discipline him for the two practices, but on the other side are you hurting the team's chances of winning by doing that, and should you have some other form of punishment to off set that.

There were times in the season where the player, through no fault of his own, had to miss maybe instead of making it to three practices leading up to the weekend, could only make one. And now you have that whole dilemma of fairness on the team. . . . those players who've been there, working hard for all three practices, this player's only been there for one practice, and yet gets to go on a road trip or gets to play their regular shift and . . . and at times . . . only a couple times during the year did that become an issue for me.

Anyway, so there was this issue: do I play them, do I not play them? Well, I didn't, but you have to weigh the effect on the entire team. Is the lesson to be learned more valuable?

Other examples of ethical issues which were shared by the coaches included: intentionally harming opponents, pushing the rules, pushing athletes, and the potential for intimate relationships developing between themselves and their athletes. The coaches who raised the issue of intentionally harming opponents did not approve of such action but saw the issue as a grey area in that the line between hurting someone and playing hard was not always clear.

I don't believe that I have ever asked a player to hurt anyone. I would ask them to go out and mark them really tightly and don't give them an inch, and they are going to clash at some stage.

If anybody's taking runs at one of our smaller players, then our bigger players, you know, nobody has to say anything, they've been brought up that way through all their [playing] that they now have to go in and make sure that doesn't happen again. It doesn't always mean they have to go in and fight. They have to go in and, face to face with that other person, say you know, basically, "stop–don't do that again, or there will be retaliation."

The grey area that exists between hurting opponents and playing hard also arises in the area of following or "pushing" the rules.

But there are a lot of grey areas in the rules in [my sport] and those grey areas are constantly being tested by players and coaches, and it's up to the referee to, you know, make those decisions when necessary.

So it [ethical issue] would be something that to me, you are asking your players to do something that goes beyond the rules of the game, but it is all in context really, my asking a player to put the ball on someone's foot to win a foul or short corner is different than going and forechecking someone in hockey. But it is all relative I guess to the sport.

As well as trying to decide how far to "push" the rules, some coaches had to consider how far one could ethically push their athletes.

My job is to push them to the limit and find out what their limits are so that I don't take them over the limits. And sometimes it happens; you do take an athlete over the limit and they get hurt and . . . and is that . . . should I be sued for that? No, I don't think so. I think . . . I think if . . . if then an athlete gets hurt and I continue to train them beyond that point, then I think that's a problem. But taking athletes to the point of injury, I don't think it's unethical.

This year, I probably let a lot go and . . . and you know, I wasn't . . . I should have been more disciplined as a coach with . . . I don't know if it's making them learn, but you know, next year.

A final potential ethical issue shared by some of the coaches was the possibility of an intimate relationship developing between the coach and the athlete. A few of the coaches saw potential dilemmas involving how actions might be perceived by athletes or outsiders.

You want to comfort the athlete or you wanna say "hey . . . good job" and you pat them on the back, you put your arm around them, or grab them by the arm, whatever. It can be perceived from the outside as sexual harassment. Now from . . . from the person that is receiving that, that may be perceived as "hey, the coach appreciates what I did," or it can be perceived as a very uncomfortable feeling. And that's what defines, I think, sexual harassment.

You know, the obvious one [ethical issue] . . . you know, if there's an attraction one way, how do you deal with it? It has to be approached in a way that, you know, that is more than just coaching. You know, you've gotta be able to define kind of the standard that you wanna operate with, and . . . and . . . explain that "hey, you know this is . . . of the situation and this is how it has to be."

As well as examples of ethical dilemmas faced by the coaches, a few of them shared some examples of "non-ethical dilemmas." These "non-issues" included the use of performance-enhancing drugs as well as alcohol, and coaches belittling athletes. Regarding performance-enhancing drug use and alcohol:

They're not gonna tell me they're doing steroids, and probably I'm not going to find out, but I may. If I find out, there's no issue. That is a rule and I have to deal with that rule. That's not debatable, you know.

We have two rules: number one, there is no alcohol on the plane there and back, for coaches or athletes, there is no alcohol in the hotel at anytime, for anybody–coaches or athletes no matter what . . . [and] there will absolutely be no parties and no girls brought back to the hotel period. . . . So we are going to avoid that issue by you not being in there. Now if that issue happens, then there is no issue here. You are wrong because you violated this code and not only would be in trouble with the University, you would be suspended by me.

A few of the coaches mentioned an issue which should be considered an ethical issue but was one which was not relevant to their situations–this involved the issue of belittling athletes.

They [some coaches] belittle their athletes and sort of degrade them at times and that's been another one [ethical dilemma] that I've had to deal with a few times.

And let the coaches who think that screaming at athletes and and pressuring them into performance and so on come out and start shouting, "it's part of the sport." There will be a lot of coaches that will stand up and would say, "no, it's not part of the sport." And it is not . . . if your philosophy is . . . is developed around that kind of approach, that you need to . . . you need to pressure the athlete, you need to belittle the athlete, you need to basically run him to the ground to get their performance out, then they're not gonna last very long.

Having considered examples of ethical issues encountered by the coaches, I will now consider the answers they gave when asked how they resolved these dilemmas.

Coaches' Resolution of Ethical Issues

When asked how they resolved the ethical issues they faced, the coaches shared a number of factors they considered when facing an ethical decision. As to be expected, the most common factors to be considered were the coach's morals/values/ethical beliefs as well as what was in the best interest of the individual athlete (recall the most common definition of an ethical issue was the tension between doing something which would be better for the team, that is, a win, or doing something which would be better for the individuals involved—including the coach, who's moral principles might be compromised if the first action was chosen). Regarding the coaches' morals/values/ethical beliefs:

I'm prepared to lose the game rather than compromise my ethical beliefs in terms of trying to win.

Well, you look at the balance of everything you know, and your values as a leader, a teacher, or a community figure, you look at what you think is pressing. You know, you have your code of ethics, and your . . . as a coach of course to follow and that you follow.

I keep referring back to what is it that . . . what is your coaching philosophy? What are your core values? And certainly you have to be considering that. If you're going against what you believe in, then that's pretty well answering your question as to what to do in your decision-making process.

My core beliefs are always gonna remain the same, because I think that they're . . . they're just . . . they are things that are integral to building blocks, to everything else. And if those building blocks are gone away, the whole foundation just crumbles, and I don't want to lose the drive to instill those core beliefs because then I can't build a strong house.

Although the coaches did not go into much detail concerning their core values and beliefs, one of their core values would have been "concern for the individual." The coaches also expressed their concern for the team, but if there was a conflict between what was best for the team and what was best for the individual athlete, the individual appeared to take priority.

> The best interest of the team, the best interests of the individual . . . what's best for that kid. . . . I think primarily I really try to take care of the individual . . . like you were them.

> You have to consider what's in the best interests of the individual and also what's in the best interest of the group or the team.

> I just know that I'm on the right way because I believe in . . . I believe in the athlete first, and . . . and I believe that they will thrive out of a healthy environment.

> [Factor to consider in resolving ethical issue] is the feelings of the athlete, obviously . . . without compromising your honesty. And you . . . you don't want to be abrupt about it. I think you . . . the facts that you want to consider are just that your end result has to be that you haven't damaged your relationship at all with, you know, the athlete in terms of coach-player, and . . . and the mutual respect that there is between both of you.

When asked about their core values, a couple of the coaches referred back to their own upbringing.

> For the most part, probably because of my background I make a lot of judgements . . . just by my own morals, you know, and upbringing.

> I was fortunate enough that my parents have taught me the basics of right and wrong, you know, it's wrong to steal, it's wrong to . . . you know.

Having considered some of the factors the coaches considered when resolving ethical issues, I turn now to a comparison of the coaches answers to the answers provided by athletes in response to similar questions.

Comparison with Athletes

It was interesting to note the differences between the athletes' and the coaches' perceptions and resolutions of ethical issues. To begin with, it was interesting to note the differences between the kinds of ethical issues shared by the coaches and those expressed by the athletes. As mentioned in chapter six, when the athletes were asked for examples of ethical issues in their sport, the examples given were whether to: play dirty, fight, trash talk, back up team mates, cut off players, and take performance-enhancing drugs. It is interesting to note how this list of examples differs from those shared by the coaches, for example, whether to: play an injured player, play a player who has missed practice, intentionally harm opponents, push the rules, push athletes, and consider the potential of an intimate relationship with an athlete.

Where there was overlap in the examples of the ethical issues arising in the sport, it was interesting to note the different perceptions of these issues by the athletes and coaches. For example, where the coaches would say that they "never told my players to hit anyone" or "never see any situations where a team will send out a player to deliberately fight a better player to take them out of the game, you know," the athletes would say:

> I don't try and hit anyone from behind, I usually try and hit fairly clean but the odd time, you know . . . it's tough to say. It depends on the circumstances and the time frame of the game.

> You don't want your best players getting injured and you have to take measures to stop that.

> Like, if you beat up the other guy, the team's going to get all, like, pumped and everything and they'll go out and score a couple goals.

The coaches and athletes obviously had different perceptions concerning the issue of fighting or playing dirty.

Regarding the issue of taking performance-enhancing drugs, the coaches did not see it as an ethical issue.

> They're not going to tell me they're doing steroids, and probably I'm not going to find out, but I may. If I find out, there's no issue. That is a rule and I have to deal with that rule. That's not debatable, you know.

It is the coach's responsibility to look after the well-being of their player and the facts are that these things are dangerous to a person's health long term or even short term and any gains, personal gains, that can be achieved by the use of performance-enhancing drugs are simple not worth the risk. It is the coach's responsibility to make or influence that decision. Like, I would not tolerate players doing that on my team.

The athletes, however, *did* see the taking of performance-enhancing drugs as a potential choice.

Guys that do drugs, or whatever steroids, I think they know it's wrong. But they're . . . they just wanna do whatever, like, to improve themselves.

Now that they recognize the strength part of it, the sport, that's where people are coming and trying to build in that area and then that's where the effects of drugs, because you don't need as much rest. You can train constantly.

Not only are there differences in the kinds of ethical issues athletes and coaches perceive in their sports (and whether an issue should be considered an ethical issue), the athletes and coaches gave different reasons for why they would make the decisions they would make regarding the issue. The reasons the athletes gave for the decisions they made could be divided into roughly six categories—reasons concerned with 1) "doing unto others as you would have them do unto you," 2) fairness, 3) respecting others, 4) not hurting the team, 5) respect for the game, and 6) fear of getting caught. The reasons the coaches gave involved a consideration of their morals/values/ethical beliefs as well as what was in the best interest of the individual athlete. The coaches also expressed their concern for the team, but if there was a conflict between what was best for the team and what was best for the individual athlete, the individual appeared to take priority.

Although the coaches did not go into much detail concerning their morals/values/ethical beliefs, there was obviously a concern for fairness when the issue of playing an athlete who had missed practice was under consideration. The issue of playing an injured athlete, as well as more general considerations of what was in the best interest of the individual, reflected a respect for others. Although the coaches did not go into as much detail as the athletes in sharing the reasons for the decisions they made, it should not be assumed that the coaches were less reflective regarding ethical decisions. What might account for the difference in the degree of detail in the reasons expressed could be that the coaches were making more assumptions when they spoke of their morals/values/ethical beliefs whereas the athletes would speak of, for example, something not being fair, rather than just subsuming fairness as one of their values.

Conceptions of Autonomy

The differences between the athletes' and the coaches' perceptions and resolutions of ethical issues ushers in the notion of autonomy. That is, how much autonomy should athletes have when it comes to identifying and dealing with ethical issues encountered in their sport? As mentioned in the introduction, a topic that arose in the interviews with the athletes concerned the influence of the coach.

> Coaches have a lot of power over you. I mean, they control who plays and who does what, and if you don't like it you can quit.

> Like, yeah . . . coaches . . . you pretty much have to take what they say.

> You have to have faith in the knowledge of your coach in order to get anywhere.

How a coach conceives of the notion of autonomy will affect whether the coach will allow his or her athletes to make autonomous ethical decisions. The coaches' answers to the question concerning how much autonomy an athlete should be given could be placed on a continuum. At one end of the continuum, there were coaches who wanted to "run the ship."

> The thing they need to understand, at least in our program and I'm sure it should be like that in every program, that there is one ship and one captain, and there may be some leeway, but the captain will eventually run the ship. And that's the way it goes. They don't have to like it, but that is the way it is going to be.

At the other end of the continuum, there were coaches who did not think the coach should single-handedly be "running the ship."

The traditional problems I believe will happen if you have just one coach and that coach drives the ship and nobody else has input into the programming. That's where . . . that's where I think teams are open to . . . and athletes are open to abuse.

I think the athlete should have a ton of autonomy in terms of ethical decisions. I mean . . . I mean, they should know . . . they should know, really understand how important doing the right thing is and understand the consequences of doing the right thing like, in a positive way . . . they should also understand the consequences of the negative things.

In between the extreme ends of the continuum, there were coaches who would give their athletes a certain degree of autonomy, but the coach still wanted a certain amount of input.

Well, they should have about fifty percent of that . . . the decision making. You know, I think you owe them as a coach . . . If he thinks a certain way, I think if you sit down with that athlete . . . I think that you have to make him sort of swing to your thinking, if you think it's unethical. But they should have, I think, about fifty percent of the say and you should be able to swing it over so that a proper ethical decision . . . by the time the conversation's over, you know.

Well, if it's a case of the injuries and their desire to play, then I . . . I think that the player should you know, have autonomy. In other situations that involve ethical dilemmas, then . . . no question that the coach should play a role in at least informing the individual to make sure that they're aware of all the facts, all of the consequences, repercussions of their decision. So I think the coach certainly has a role to play . . . a huge role there to play in providing information. And then it's up to the . . . I think the player should have that autonomy.

Although the coaches in the study were not asked for their conceptions of autonomy, one can infer their underlying conceptions of autonomy from the answers they gave concerning the question of how much autonomy athletes should be given.

A number of philosophers make a distinction between two fundamentally different notions of autonomy.[1] In Michael Meyer's words:

The first view might be called negative autonomy: an autonomous person is *not* directed by another. The second view could be called positive autonomy: an autonomous person *is* actively self-directed. One might better distinguish these two positions by noting that negative autonomy is a social conception, a conception of liberty. On the other hand, positive autonomy involves having a certain relationship with the "natural" world of one's own emotions and desires.[2]

As Joseph Kupfer points out, "It is not enough simply to be free from others' interference; autonomy requires awareness of control over one's relation to others, including their access to us."[3] Thomas May refers to these different notions of autonomy as "autonomy as autarkeia [or self-sufficiency]" and "autonomy as self-rule."[4] According to May, the notion of autonomy as autarkeia has a long history, going back to Aristotle, then Kant, and more recently Joel Feinberg, John Rawls and Robert Paul Wolff. Aristotle saw autarkeia, or self-sufficiency, as the primary good and chief aim of a city-state: "Again, the object for which a thing exists, its end, is its chief good; and self sufficiency is an end, and a chief good."[5] Kant discusses autonomy in terms of moral value. He viewed the presence of the will as not being dependent on external considerations for its moral value. "Autonomy of the will is the property the will has of being a law to itself (independently of any property of the objects of volition)."[6]

The Kantian view of moral autonomy as autarkeia has influenced more recent work on the topic. May notes that Feinberg's four related meanings of autonomy: the capacity to govern oneself, the actual condition of self-government, an ideal of character derived from that condition; or the sovereign authority to govern oneself, involve the core concept of "self-sufficiency."

> That the idea of self-sufficiency could be seen as a core concept is particularly plausible when one considers that Feinberg especially stresses self-sufficiency in his discussion of autonomy as an "actual condition" and as an "ideal of character." This is important, since it seems that it is the actual condition of autonomy that the other uses of autonomy revolve around. For example, a capacity for autonomy is a capacity to realize the actual condition of autonomy. The sovereign authority, or right to autonomy is a right to the actual condition of self-government; and the ideal of character is described by Feinberg as derived from the actual condition of autonomy. Thus, the "actual condition" of autonomy plays a central role in all four concepts, and the emphasis on self-sufficiency here should carry over to the other concepts as well.[7]

Rawls also places an emphasis on "self-sufficiency" when he proposes that one's life should be governed by judgments that are "independent of natural contingencies and accidental circumstances."[8] Hence, he proposes that people test their actions against principles adopted behind the "veil of ignorance." Finally, Wolff states that "[t]he autonomous man, insofar as he is autonomous, is not subject to the will of another. He may do what another tells him, but not *because* he has been told to do it."[9]

In contrast to the notion of autonomy as autarkeia or self-sufficiency, the notion of autonomy as self-rule allows for the incorporation of external influences into a person's determination of action. John Macken traces the use of the term "autonomy" to the Greeks who would denote certain rights to the city-state even when the city-state was dependent on a mother-city or outside power. This notion of "autonomy" remained throughout the Enlightenment when reference was made to the rights of individuals to manage their own affairs within the limits of a larger framework set by law. The word "autonomy" is actually derived from the Greek words *autos* and *nomos* which means "self-rule." It is ironic that Aristotle, who claimed that autarkeia, or self-sufficiency is the primary good and chief aim of a city-state, presents an analogy of city-states as ships, with the citizens being sailors and the ruler the helmsman.[10] May argues that the analogy of ships and helmsman [helmsperson] is an apt analogy for the notion of autonomy as "self-rule." What distinguishes Aristotle's use of the ship analogy from May's is the issue of how the helmsperson reacts to the external factors.

Aristotle, unlike Kant, admitted that external factors are incorporated into the determination of moral duty. Returning to the ship analogy, these external factors would be comparable to weather and currents, and so forth. Aristotle did not see these external factors as threats to one's ability to rule as long as one acted according to practical wisdom. As May points out:

> To understand practical wisdom in Aristotle is to understand determination of virtuous action as involving a guide to action in relation to the external considerations of one's own capabilities and characteristics, as well as the situation at hand. Practical wisdom determines virtuous action but does so in the context of the circumstances of the individual.[11]

In Aristotle's own words:

> The general account being of this nature, the account of particular cases is yet more lacking in exactness; for they do not fall under any art or precept

but the agents themselves must in each case consider what is appropriate to the occasion, as happens also in the art of medicine or of *navigation* (italics added).[12]

Thus, according to Aristotle, external influences would not determine behavior, but rather affect how one rules. However, May points out that some external influences have more "influence" than others, for example, a gunman putting a gun to the head of a victim and ordering her to walk across the street. Aristotle also acknowledges such situations (in keeping with the ship analogy): "Something of the sort happens also with regard to the throwing of goods overboard in a storm; for in the abstract no one throws goods away voluntarily, but on condition of securing the safety of himself and his crew any sensible man does so."[13] Thus, we have a standard of autonomy. In May's words:

> Nonetheless, a standard does exist: does the behavior reflect the agent's evaluative assessment, or are the circumstances such that no sensible man could choose otherwise, so that the determination of action reflects the circumstances more than the agent's evaluative assessment. If it is the former, the agent acts as helmsman. If it is the latter, the ship's course reflects more the external circumstances than the agent's practical wisdom.[14]

This standard differs from the notion of autonomy as autarkeia in that the determination of one's action is not made in a detached or self-sufficient manner. As May points out, "Autonomy does not require detachment from external influences. Rather, it requires that the agent actively assess these influences rather than simply react to them. External influences do not *cause* action, but rather provide information that the agent, as 'helmsman,' then steers according to."[15] Accepting the notion of autonomy as self-rule as opposed to self-sufficiency does not achieve Kant's desire to view people as purely ends and not means, but it does not leave us as means in a Humean "slave to the passions" vein. Once again, in May's words:

> By positing man's judgment as helmsman, we understand the action as a means to an end whose direction is set by the agent himself. While this direction is set in light of considerations many of which are beyond the agent's control, the direction itself is not simply a product of these factual considerations, but a product of the agent's active assessment of factual

information. . . . This is all we require for a plausible conception of autonomy.[16]

I would concur with May that the notion of autonomy as self-rule is a plausible conception of autonomy, and further, such a conception has significant implications for the coach-athlete relationship.

Coach-Athlete Relationship

How a coach conceives of autonomy will affect how much autonomy the athlete holds in the coach-athlete relationship. The coach might conceive of autonomy as "self-sufficiency" and thus deny his or her athletes any degree of autonomy. Or the coach may conceive of autonomy as "self-rule" with the athlete being the "helmsperson" and the coach being one of the external considerations the athlete must take into account when making ethical decisions. I will look at each of these conceptions of autonomy and how they would translate into the coach-athlete relationship.

It is ironic that the coaches in this study who did not want to grant their athletes much autonomy used the ship analogy.

> The thing they need to understand, at least in our program and I'm sure it should be like that in every program, that there is one ship and one captain, and there may be some leeway, but the captain will eventually run the ship. And that's the way it goes. They don't have to like it, but that is the way it is going to be.

What is important to remember here is that the "helmsperson" is the coach, not the athlete. In fairness to the coaches who would adopt this conception of autonomy (or rather, lack thereof on the part of the athlete), we would be justified in assuming that the athletes' interests and desires would be considered as one of the external factors considered in making ethical decisions (recall that the most common definition of an ethical dilemma was the tension between doing something which would be better for the team, i.e., a win, or doing something which would be better for the individuals involved–including the coach, who's moral principles might be compromised if the first action was chosen). However, the coach would have the "final say" under this conception of autonomy as "self-sufficiency."

If coaches adopted the conception of autonomy as "self-rule," with the athlete as "helmsperson," the situation would be quite different.

> I think the athlete should have a ton of autonomy in terms of ethical decisions. I mean . . . I mean, they should know . . . they should know, really understand how important doing the right thing is and understand the consequences of doing the right thing like, in a positive way. . . . They should also understand the consequences of the negative things.

In the situation of athlete as "helmsperson," the coach would be one of the external considerations the athlete would take into account when making ethical decisions. But as May suggested, the agent [in this case, the athlete] would actively assess the influence [in this case, the coach's influence] rather than simply react to it. "External influences do not *cause* action, but rather provide information that the agent, as 'helmsman,' then steers according to."[17] One of the coaches interviewed acknowledged the role of the coach as "information provider."

> Well, if it's a case of the injuries and their desire to play, then I . . . I think that the player should you know, have autonomy. In other situations that involve ethical dilemmas, then . . . no question that the coach should play a role in at least informing the individual to make sure that they're aware of all the facts, all of the consequences, repercussions of their decision. So I think the coach certainly has a role to play . . . a huge role there to play in providing information. And then it's up to the . . . I think the player should have that autonomy.

Viewing the coach as "information provider" parallels the situation of informed consent in medicine. Kenneth Ravizza and Kathy Daruty consider informed consent in medicine and suggest an analogous situation for athletics.

> In an effort to develop the structure of a realistic and practical informed consent for athletics, full disclosure should be made to athletes in three basic areas:
> 1.   The nature of the coach's philosophy or attitude related to coaching a particular sport;
> 2.   Current information about the risks, complications, and benefits associated with the specific aspects of participation in that sport;
> 3.   Recognition that feasible alternatives may exist to the coach's position in certain situations and the athlete is responsible for

communicating reasons for a change in the team plan or individual strategy as it relates to training and performance.[18]

Regarding the first area, if the coach's philosophy involves screaming and yelling "to get the most out of" his or her athletes, if the athlete is informed of this, he or she can expect that behavior and if unable to accept it, choose to play elsewhere. The second area, concerning risks and complications pertains particularly to the area of injuries (recall that whether to play injured athletes was one of the most frequently cited ethical dilemmas shared by the coaches interviewed). If athletes are given all of the information concerning the risks of playing with their injury, they can make informed decisions, taking some of the pressure off the coach. "A truly informed disclosure has many advantages, not the least of which is a reduction of the coach's stress, as responsibility for the athlete's performance is placed upon both the athlete and the coach."[19] The third area, concerning alternatives to the coach's position, requires an emphasis on communication between the coach and the athletes.

> The point here is that the coach and the athlete share a responsibility to communicate regularly. Flexibility is the nature of competitive situations, but most coaches are unwilling to allow last-minute changes in a tried and tested game plan unless there is a good reason. We have argued that the essence of informed consent in athletics is the coach's responsibility to ensure that there are no suprises during the season; however, the corollary is that athletes cannot expect last-minute flexibility in the absence of a regular ongoing communication with the coach. This continuing communication builds a bond between athlete and coach that ultimately results in mutual respect.[20]

Respect for the coach requires not only ongoing communication, but also the recognition that the coach is knowledgeable about his or her sport. This situation ushers in one final issue, the importance of being *an* authority and not just *in* authority. "Being in authority is to be placed in a socially sanctioned role, which carries with it certain rights and responsibilities. . . . Someone who is *an* authority is someone who is an expert in some area of knowledge or skill."[21] Thus, a coach is in a position of authority, "a socially sanctioned role," but he or she also needs to be *an* authority in the sense of having the requisite knowledge and skill necessary to provide the information the athlete needs to make informed decisions in the playing of his or her sport. With a coach who is an authority, who seeks informed consent from his or her athletes, the athletes will find themselves in a position where they can grow, not only as athletes, but as autonomous individuals.

Chapter 8

The Relationship Between Coaching and Teaching

In chapter seven, the issue of autonomy and athletes was examined. I argued that athletes should have a certain degree of positive autonomy. The development of autonomous individuals is an important aim of the educational enterprise. Coaches should view themselves more as teachers and encourage the development of autonomy in their athletes. There are also other attributes which are typically perceived as belonging to teachers which coaches should adopt, and vice versa. This chapter will involve an examination of these attributes, and in so doing, attempt to narrow the gap between sport and physical education.

Coaching and teaching are typically viewed as distinct professions with distinct goals. This distinction is perhaps most evident in sports circles, where the coach, although his/her job entails to a large degree the teaching of skills, technique and strategy, is always referred to as "the coach" and never "a teacher." I am not certain whether it is this distinction between coach and teacher which creates the resulting distinction between sports and physical education, or whether it is the assumed differences between sports and physical education which have created the "coach" not "teacher" attitude prevalent in sports circles. The purpose of this chapter is to look at the relationship between sport and physical education and in so doing, examine the relationship between coaching and teaching. By looking at the content of physical education and sports programs and the methods by which this content is engaged in, and by expanding our conception of coaching to include attributes which we typically view as having to do with the "educational enterprise," coaching and sport will be the better for it. Likewise, physical education must take seriously the teaching of sport as the competitive activity it is meant to be, if physical education is to fulfill its role as an educative activity.

In order to examine the relationship between sport and physical education, two other distinctions must also be addressed: the distinction between education and training, and the distinction between education and competition. In considering the differences between education and training, some distinctions that are typically made in relation to education and training should be dissolved; that being, the distinction between knowledge and skill, and the distinction between theory and practice. In examining the relationship between education and competition, education and competition should not be viewed as antithetical, as some educators would advocate, but rather, competition is a necessary part of education. Before examining any of these distinctions, it is first necessary to clarify what we mean by sport and physical education.

Sport and Physical Education

Sport is typically perceived as a socially constructed activity which has an element of physicality as well as competition. Although some sports are less physical than others, for example, archery as opposed to football, and some activities usually denoted as sport do not seem to have obvious competitors, for example, mountain climbing or kayaking, I will make the assumption that there must be some degree of physicality and competition for an activity to be deemed a "sport". The description of sport as a "socially constructed" activity is important for our comparison of sport and physical education. What I mean by "socially constructed" is the fact that sport activities operate within a context where goals are determined, for example, to put a ball through a hoop while defending yourself against an opposing team who also wants to put a ball through their hoop; and rules are constructed to regulate the achievements of those goals, for example, you cannot touch a member of the opposing team. The fact that sport activities operate within a "closed system;" that is, goals are created and then rules developed for the achieving of those goals, implies that sports are in some way "hived off" from the rest of life's activities. This is in stark contrast to the goals of the "education enterprise."

When referring to physical education, I have in mind a subject area that is part of a larger education project. Although in this postmodern age, the Petersian conception of a liberal education is considered by many to be passé, I argued in chapter two that the choice of an educational curriculum cannot "get off the ground" unless students are engaged in activities whose aim is the development of rationality. The development of rationality requires the acquisition of knowledge with which one can be rational about. In Peters's words: "[I]t is equally absurd to foster an abstract skill called 'critical thinking' [I would agree with Siegel who views critical thinking as the educational cognate of rationality] without handing on anything concrete to be critical about."[1] Although Peters did not include physical education in the forms of knowledge he thought should be handed on to students, I argued in chapter one that the practical knowledge involved in the teaching and learning of physical education activities is an important component of a liberal education. I will examine in more detail what is involved in the acquisition of practical knowledge in a later section of this chapter. At this point, we must consider what is involved in an education as opposed to a training experience.

Training and Education

Once again, I must acknowledge Peters's work when considering the distinction between education and training. "The hypothesis to be tested is that 'trained' suggests the development of competence in a limited skill or mode of thought whereas 'educated' suggests a linkage with a wider system of beliefs."[2] Peters cites the example of "educating" rather than "training" emotions. "This is surely because the different emotions are differentiated by their cognitive core, by the different beliefs that go with them."[3] The importance of beliefs will be examined in a later section when I discuss the beliefs involved in acquiring practical knowledge in physical education programs. In referring to "training" the emotions, Peters points out that this situation occurs when we want people not to give way to a particular emotion.

> There is no suggestion of transforming a person's appraisal of a situation by working on his beliefs; rather of developing fairly standardized appraisals such as those connected with pity, anger, and fear in relation to appropriate objects and of not feeling such emotions so strongly that he is overcome by them.[4]

The distinction between educating and training emotions also demonstrates the importance of a specific "end" for a training exercise.

The general point that is illustrated by these examples [educating and training the emotions] is that the concept of "training" has application when a skill or competence has to be acquired which is to be exercised in relation to a specific end or function or in accordance with the canons of some specific mode of thought, or practice.[5]

The notion of a specific end as a result of training can be applied readily to the sport context. For example, there are more efficient ways than others to strike or catch a ball, and it makes sense to strive for that specific end (the efficient way to strike or catch a ball). It is examples such as these which lead people to associate coaching with training as opposed to educating. Martin Lee alludes to this association in his distinction between physical education and sport: "The former is considered to be more about personal development while the latter focuses on the development of excellence in physical skills and their testing in competition."[6] Is this dichotomy between training and educating an appropriate one for the dichotomy which appears to exist between coaching and teaching? Or, perhaps the application of the training/educating dichotomy does more harm than good concerning coaching and teaching.

Coaching as Training and Teaching as Educating?

As noted in the beginning of this chapter, there is typically a marked distinction made between the professions of coaching and teaching. This perceived distinction is evident in much sociological and psychological work on the topic of teacher/coach role conflicts.[7] In the study conducted by D. Chu, respondents were asked to indicate the skill perceived to be the most important for teaching and coaching. Communication skills were ranked first for teaching and subject matter knowledge ranked first for coaching. The importance of subject matter knowledge was echoed in a study of basketball coach John Wooden: "[W]e can state that at least 75 percent of Wooden's teaching acts carry information. This information density is clearly a significant feature of his success."[8] In a study conducted by Linda Bain and Janice Wendt, they found that communication skills were ranked as important for both teachers and coaches. However, they found a difference regarding the ability to motivate students to achieve, in that such a characteristic was ranked as more important for coaching than for teaching. The importance placed on coaches having sufficient subject matter knowledge as well as the ability to motivate students to achieve should not be suprising when we consider the goals of most sports programs as opposed to physical education programs.

> The instructional physical education program should be a daily, required, diversified program for the entire student body, whereas the interscholastic sports program is an opportunity for interested and highly-skilled athletes to practice specific sports and compete with other trained athletes from other schools.[9]

As mentioned in the beginning of this chapter, competition is an integral part of sport. It is this aspect of sport that often becomes the focal point of sport and also the clashing point between education and sport. Janet Ashburn, in comparing the teaching that occurs in physical education as opposed to sport, "maintains a clear distinction between the two types of teaching: one is educational and the other is for competition."[10] I will examine the importance of competition for sport and physical education in the following section.

Another distinction that is frequently made between coaching and teaching was alluded to in the previous section. Training is typically perceived as developing competence in a limited skill where education is viewed as a "wider" process involving connections with a wider system of beliefs. This distinction would seem to apply to the coaching/teaching professions in that coaches do typically develop skills limited to a particular sport to a particular group of athletes. As L. Hendry points out: "[T]he coach can operate basically to produce competitive excellence within a limited sphere of physical activities with a relatively small group of athletes."[11] Teaching, on the other hand, aims at developing all domains of all children.

> [T]hrough physical education[,] three areas are inter-twined: the affective, the cognitive, and the psychomotor. In physical education, an attempt is made to target all three areas for improvement as a tool for educating the "whole person." Sport, in contrast, claims to affect these areas also yet does not specifically focus on all three areas within the context of an activity.[12]

Whether this "narrow" sport focus as opposed to a "wider" educational focus is a good thing is the topic of the following section.

Coaches as Teachers

Although the distinction between training and educating would seem to apply to the professions of coaching and teaching respectively, such a distinction does more harm than good and it would be helpful to dissolve the dichotomy between training and educating when applied to sport and physical education. The fact that coaches work with fewer people and at a higher skill level does not negate the fact that they are engaged in teaching–teaching their athletes skills, technique and strategy.

> Whether teaching or coaching, physical and sports activity is the medium used to teach and educate students. Whether working with students in the class setting or on the practice field/court, the objectives and goals, depending upon the situation, should only differ in degree.[13]

When the coach perceives what he or she does as teaching, perhaps the idea of educating the whole person might come into play. Coaches typically view their task as involving the development of physical skills and technique, with some concern for strategy involving the cognitive domain, but usually ignoring the affective domain.

> Training, or coaching, children in sport can be considered to be an educational activity. The two processes need not necessarily conflict even though training and coaching may be directed primarily toward developing better performance in a particular activity and education is normally considered to be concerned with the development of people. However, training can be educational if it is conducted in such a way that it contributes to the total development of the person.[14]

It is ironic that coaching typically places almost sole emphasis on the psychomotor domain and some emphasis on the cognitive domain. The fact that coaches usually have fewer numbers of people they work with, as well as the fact that coaches will often spend far more time with their athletes, than teachers with their students, would seem to result in a situation conducive to helping athletes develop in the affective domain.

Shifting the coach's mindset from training to educating would also facilitate viewing the coach's job, not only as the development of "narrow" skill acquisition, but also an activity connected with a wider set of beliefs.

I suggest that the most daunting problems with which we have to deal are those that have not yet been tackled anything like seriously enough in any of the coaching schemes I know. I see these as arising in and from our consideration of what principles we *ought* to follow in our regulation of our affairs in promotion of the forms of excellence embodied and exemplified in the games that we play. These are the problems of ethics and, crucially, of metaphysics–questions to do with such issues as what view of the nature of Man we adopt and what version we have of the best forms of social setting in which athletes can best develop their own personal identity, the particular centres of consciousness that is them and all their main concerns, and how best we may institutionalize the (political) arrangements and social relations that are most likely to promote optimum development of that.[15]

Expanding the coach's job to include an awareness of ethical issues involved in sport will not only benefit the athletes but also the practice of sport itself.

One final area where a shift from training to education in the coaching discipline would have positive results, concerns not the content of what is being taught, as much as the method by which skills and technique are acquired. An important aspect of educating the "whole person" is respect for the student as an autonomous individual.[16] Although an emphasis on developing students' autonomy is not always found in educational institutions, it is found even less often on the sports field (as noted in chapter seven). In the words of a basketball coach:

Do we give our athletes credit for thinking, or are we too busy telling them over and over again "how it's done"? All coaches find themselves becoming irritated at athletes' so-called inability to think for themselves, but have we given them the opportunity to develop this very important characteristic?[17]

One of the reasons why an education context may be more conducive to the development of autonomy than a sport context, has to do with the content of each activity. As mentioned previously, in a sporting context, there is more appropriate ways than others to strike or catch a ball, and so forth. Thus, there might appear less reason to allow an athlete the opportunity to make autonomous choices. An education context, where the focus is on a wider set of beliefs (or, as I will argue in the following section, intentional actions), is more conducive to the student making autonomous choices. However, the fact that there is a more appropriate way than another to perform certain physical skills does not preclude the coach from having the athletes question why this is so. This questioning, or as I argued in chapter three, critical thinking, is fundamental to the development of autonomy in both students and athletes. Also fundamental to the development of autonomy is the encouraging of responsibility on the part of the athlete or student. This would require a shift from viewing the coach or teacher as "the one with all the answers."

> If coaches embrace the objective of helping athletes to become more responsible, they should view their role as being available to the athlete when needed, assisting when the athlete recognizes the need for assistance, and minimizing the athlete's dependency on the coach. Such an approach places emphasis on athletes becoming responsible for the learning of skills rather than on coaches being responsible for teaching skills.[18]

Advocating the development of autonomous thinking skills, giving attention to a wider set of beliefs, including those concerned with the affective domain, and encouraging responsibility on the part of the athlete, might place some coaches in a state of tension. "In the contemporary situation, a coach who is centrally concerned with the total development of his youthful charges will face some formidable challenges and real pressures."[19] A very real pressure faced by many coaches is the pressure to win. It may be justifiable in the professional sports domain to tie a coach's job to his or her performance, but unfortunately, many coaches' jobs in educational institutions are also tied to their "win-loss" record. It is beyond the scope of this chapter to make further distinctions between and justifications for professional, amateur and school sport, but suffice it to say, such distinctions are important when examining the relationship between coaching and teaching.

> To fulfill themselves as teachers, coaches must offset the powerful pro model, withstand unreasonable outside pressures, and understand that their players are not full-time athletes. They must reinforce on a daily basis the long-standing, uncommercial rewards of sports.[20]

Suggesting that coaches must offset the pressure to win does not negate the importance of competition. However, it is important to illuminate the goal of competition. The professional model, where jobs and salaries are typically tied to "win-loss" records, can often result in a "win-at-all costs" mentality. Unfortunately, this mentality often surfaces in the amateur and school ranks. If the "win-at-all costs" attitude can be separated from the concept of competition, competition should play an important role in physical education as well as sport programs.

Physical Education and Competition

Having suggested ways in which coaches should perceive themselves as teachers, I now want to consider an area where teachers should view themselves in what is typically considered to be the coach's domain–the advocate of competitive sports. There has been a recent move in physical education curriculum design to incorporate a sport education model.[21] "Despite debates about the potential of sport to be miseducative, we continue to promote sport education because of its educative potential in a number of areas of learning and also because of the cultural significance of sport."[22] The sport education model differs from institutionalized sport in three distinct ways: participation requirements, developmentally appropriate competition, and diverse roles.[23] In sport education, teams are kept small, there are no elimination formats, and all students play equally and have equal opportunity to learn position play. Sport forms used in sport education are matched to the developmental level of the students. "While playing hard and fairly to win is stressed, the dominating 'ethic' of sport education is to take part fairly and to improve individual and team performance."[24] Finally, in sport education, students not only play the performer's role, they also take on the diverse roles of referee, scorekeeper, coach, manager, trainer, statistician, publicity officer, and sports board members (these positions would be rotated as the seasons and sports changed). "As students learn roles and become more responsible for their own sport experiences, the managerial and 'traffic-director' role for the teacher diminishes. Also, students acquire knowledge and develop attitudes that will make them more informed participants in adult sport cultures."[25]

The benefits of mass participation in sport, playing hard and fairly, and becoming informed participants of adult sport cultures will still be countered by educationists who see competition as psychologically damaging and unhealthy.[26] However, not only does competitive sport have the benefits suggested by advocates of the sport education model, competition is indispensible to the acquisition of practical knowledge which, as argued in chapter one, is fundamental to the physical education enterprise. In referring to "practical knowledge," I do not want to be mistaken for supporting the theory/practice or knowledge/skill distinctions. "Practical knowledge" is not simply the practice of some theoretical proposition, or some skill distinct from knowledge. Rather, practical knowledge is a form of knowledge in its own right. As noted in chapter four, the acquisition of practical knowledge requires some means to assess whether the student can exhibit recognizable success at whatever skill is being learned. I argued that this assessment is best facilitated through comparison with others in competitive activities. A key point in my argument for the fundamental role of competitive activities in physical education is the notion of competition as "striving together." This "striving together" necessitates a respect for one's opponents. Rather than avoiding competitive activities because of the potential for disrespecting opponents, the necessity for moral education becomes evident. Thus, rather than considering competition to be psychologically damaging and unhealthy, educationists should focus on the importance of moral education in the physical education program, thus allowing for the possibility of positive competitive experiences.

The Relationship between Physical Education and Sport

Having examined, albeit briefly, what is involved in physical education and sport, as well as argued against viewing coaching as training and teaching as educating, it seems important to conclude this chapter by explicating the relationship between physical education and sport. Suggesting that coaches should expand their notion of coaching to include the wider focus usually attributed to teaching, and that teachers should adopt the positive attitude toward competition which is usually held by coaches, appears to be advocating the narrowing of the gap between coaching and teaching—or, physical education and sports. Narrowing the gap would be a good thing and both sport and physical education programs would benefit from these expanded perceptions. However, sport is not the same as physical education and physical education is not the same as sport. The main difference between these two activities lies in their function in society. As I argued in chapter two, education has to do with the development of rationality, and acquiring knowledge, both theoretical and practical, is essential for this development. Sport, unlike education, is a socially constructed activity, which is "hived off" from other life activities. However, being socially constructed and hived off from other life activities does not make sport unimportant. On the contrary, sport is a unique aspect of our humanness.

> If sport as a symbolic language provides a way to experience a unique aspect of one's humanness, and if it provides opportunities for feelings of authenticity, then it is justified in the culture. And if education is seen as providing opportunities for bringing students to a total knowledge of what it is to be human, sport is a necessity in the educational curriculum, for it concentrates on an aspect of man no other symbolic language approaches.[27]

Thus, sport is seen as the content for physical education programs. However, physical education programs could, and should, involve more than sport. Human movement is a part of all sports, but it is also a part of the activity of dance. Students should be exposed to both the functional and expressive aspects of human movement.[28] Dance, in particular creative dance,[29] gives students the opportunity to use movement in a more expressive manner than that usually allowed for in sport, that is, it does not matter *how* one gets the ball through the hoop, but it does matter how a dancer moves his or her arm, for example, a fast movement will "say" something different than a slow movement. Thus, a well balanced physical education program should include sports and dance.

Just as physical education programs involve more than sports, sport programs are not solely educational. In fact, after athletes have acquired the practical knowledge necessary for their sport, sport might take on a different function. However, as long as athletes are participating in what Simon refers to as the "quest for excellence,"[30] there will always be an educational element in their pursuit. That is, athletes will want to continue to acquire practical knowledge in their sport and continue seeking out competitors to gauge their success in the knowledge they have acquired. As argued in chapter two, the acquisition of knowledge is intrinsic to what it means to be educated. However, sport can, and often is, played for more instrumental reasons, that is, for fun, as in recreational sport, or for money, as in professional sport. I am not suggesting that recreational or professional sport is inferior to sport played for the intrinsic value of acquiring and perfecting practical knowledge. However, these different functions of sport clarify the educational or non-educational emphasis in sport. Although sport can be more than education and physical education can be more than sport, I must reiterate the commonalities between sport and physical education, for these commonalities have significant implications for the professions of coaching and teaching.

Chapter 9

Physical Education, Sport and Aesthetic Experience

In chapter eight I proposed narrowing the gap between coaching and teaching. However, I do recognize that sport and physical education have different functions in our society. I acknowledged that not all sport is education, for example, recreational and professional sport, and that physical education is not simply sport. Human movement involves both functional and expressive aspects,[1] and thus, a well-balanced physical education program should include both functional and expressive movement. Although physical educators might think that the expressive aspect of movement can be experienced through what has been referred to as "aesthetic sports,"[2] there are important differences between so called "aesthetic sports" and what I would argue are truly aesthetic activities such as dance.

"That was a beautiful shot" or "what a graceful dismount" are common utterances heard at basketball games or gymnastics competitions. Talk of beauty and grace in reference to sport is not new. The philosophy of sport literature includes numerous articles that connect aesthetics with sport.[3] Most of the scholars who have written in this area take it for granted that there is a connection between aesthetics and sport. Their work typically "fleshes out" what this connection entails. Although I would agree that there are some commonalities between aesthetics and sports (e.g., emphasis on form, visions of beauty, etc.), the contrasts outweigh the commonalities. However, delineating the distinctions between aesthetics and sport should not be perceived as a negative move, but rather, such a project highlights what is fundamental and significant to aesthetic activity as separate from what is fundamental and significant to sport. I will first consider some perspectives on aesthetics and then examine what it is about sport that tempts us to refer to such activity as aesthetic.

Aesthetics "Proper"

The realm of aesthetics is one that encompasses a variety of perspectives, from analytic to postmodern thought. One of the first analytic philosophers to advance a serious analysis of aesthetic response was J. O. Urmson. He proposed that the criterion for distinguishing an aesthetic response from other kinds of responses lay in the kind of reasons given for the response. He gives the example of someone gaining satisfaction from a play. If the playhouse is full and the person watching the play has financed it, the satisfaction would probably be economic. If the person watching the play feels that the play will have an improving effect on the audience, the satisfaction could be considered moral.[4] An aesthetic response, on the other hand, would involve a response to the form and content of the play. John Hospers argues that the whole concept of aesthetic experience is confused and that it is extremely difficult to distinguish aesthetic experience from moral, religious, intellectual or sexual experience. Kingsley Price argues that the "question 'What makes an experience aesthetic?' asks not what makes the awareness in an aesthetic experience aesthetic since that cannot be a question, but what makes the object in an aesthetic experience an aesthetic object."[5] Focus on the aesthetic object is evident in the work of Michael Mitias, who argues against Hosper's view that the concept of an aesthetic experience is untenable. Mitias defines an aesthetic experience via the aesthetic qualities possessed by an object:

> [O]n the basis of my experience and the testimony of art critics and philosophers I can, however, say that though rich in its scope, appeal, and depth the aesthetic quality appears to have a general identity in all the arts, and art works: regardless of its habitat–a poem, a novel, a statue, a dance, a building, a symphony or a film–aesthetic quality belongs to the art works as a potentiality, i.e., as a human aspect that can be actualized as meaning in the aesthetic experience.[6]

The notion of aesthetic quality involving potentiality for meaning is reiterated in the work of Abbs. Contrary to the conception of "art for art's sake," Abbs advocates art for meaning's sake.[7] By "art for meaning's sake," Abbs is referring to the potential for people to derive meaning from encounters with art. Abbs refers to the aesthetic as "*a particular form of sensuous understanding*, a mode of apprehending through the senses the patterned import of human experience."[8] I have argued elsewhere[9] that the apprehension of the sensuous as it pertains to experiences of the senses is a necessary condition for having an aesthetic experience. However, such perceptive experiences, be they visual, oral, tactile, and so forth, are not sufficient for an aesthetic experience to occur. Also needed for an aesthetic experience is the involvement of feelings on the part of the participant. This involvement of feelings is part of the sensuous in the definition of aesthetic as sensuous understanding. It is interesting to note the linguistic connections between sensation and feeling. Abbs provides some illuminating illustrations. "'To keep in touch' is both to keep in contact and to remain close in feeling. To *touch* an object is to have a perceptual experience; *to be touched* by an event is to be emotionally moved by it. To have a *tactile* experience is to have a sensation in the finger-tips; to show *tact* is to exhibit an awareness of the feelings of others."[10]

Both the employment of the senses and the experiencing of feelings are necessary for an aesthetic experience to occur. The final condition necessary for an aesthetic experience involves understanding, that is, Abbs's "sensuous *understanding*." The apprehension through the senses (including feeling) makes it possible to attain sensuous understanding of the human experience. How is this possible? The art historian E. H. Gombrich proposes some possible answers. Gombrich traces the history of representative painting by analyzing image-making. He suggests that artists "make" not "match" images. "What [artists] had to learn before they could create an illusion of reality was not to 'copy what they saw' but to manipulate those ambiguous cues on which we have to rely in stationary vision till their image was indistinguishable from reality."[11] Thus, "What a painter inquires into is not the nature of the physical world but the nature of our reactions to it."[12] It is not only the artist's reaction to the physical world that is the basis of artistic inquiry, but also the reaction of the audience. In reference to Renaissance art, Gombrich states that "[i]t is clear that an entirely new idea of art is taking shape here. It is an art in which the painter's skill in suggesting must be matched by the public's skill in taking hints. . . The willing beholder responds to the artist's suggestion because he enjoys the transformation that occurs in front of his eyes."[13] It is the acquaintance with a "transformed" world that can lead to an enriched understanding of the human experience. As Rosalind Hursthouse so aptly put it, "They [artists] can also reveal how they think, consciously or unconsciously, about things by what they represent and the ways in which they do it. This can make us think differently, and, again because of the way in which 'interpretation' and 'reception' are interdependent, this may lead us to see differently."[14] A good example of "seeing the world differently" concerns the area of moral truths in works of art. As Tom Sorell suggests, "[I]t is possible to hold that through works such as novels we enlarge the range of people we can empathize with, the range of situations we can imaginatively project ourselves into, and therefore the perspectives from which we can assess the rightness of actions or ways of life that we otherwise would never have thought twice about."[15]

Another way of looking at an artist's transformation of the world and the enriched understanding gained by the audience as a result of apprehending the artist's work, is to view the process as a communication of an artist's "discovery." H. Keller gives the example of an artist painting a picture of a mountain:

> The purpose of the picture of the mountain is communication. It is an attempt on the part of the artist to get something across–a discovery of his own. Nor is he just communicating what he feels about the mountain; he expresses something which we all feel about it–without our having been conscious of it prior to the emergence of his work of art.[16]

In using the term "communication" to describe what is happening between the artist and the audience, we must be careful not to think of communication in purely discursive terms. Jacques Maquet makes a distinction between receivers of linguistic messages and beholders of art.

> Receivers of linguistic messages–the readers of this page, for instance–apprehend meanings embodied in the words, sentences, and texts by the sender–the writer of this book, for instance–ideally without adding anything to them. . . . Beholders, on the contrary, invest the visual object with meanings related, in part, to their past experiences. Because of this rooting in individual experiences, symbolic meanings attributed to the same object by different beholders are bound to be different. However, this symbolic variety is limited.

The variety of aesthetic responses is limited for a couple of reasons. One, which Maquet points out, is that the commonalities in our experiences are many. Another limiting factor concerns the artist's intention. In Maquet's words, "[A] beholder's interpretation of a visual work is valid for the beholder if it has the quality of compelling evidence."[18] "Compelling evidence" includes the recognition of the formal features the artist has chosen to express the experience he or she is expressing. A more detailed exploration of aesthetic form and content arises in an examination of the distinction between the aesthetic and the artistic.

A criticism that may be raised concerning the previous discussion is that I have conflated the aesthetic and the artistic. A response to this criticism requires a closer look at potentially competing conceptions of the aesthetic. Best distinguishes the aesthetic from the artistic by suggesting that the "aesthetic applies, for instance, to sunsets, birdsong and mountain ranges, whereas the artistic tends to be limited, at least in its central uses, to artifacts or performances intentionally created by man."[19] According to Best, "[T]he arts are characteristically concerned with contemporary moral, social, political and emotional issues. Yet this is not true of the aesthetic."[20] Best's definitions of the aesthetic and artistic might appear to be in conflict with Abbs's definition of the aesthetic as "sensuous understanding,"[21] for upon first glance, sunsets do not seem to have much to contribute to an understanding of the human experience. However, a closer look at the sunset experience is in order here. At times, when confronted with a beautiful sunset, a person simply enjoys the colors, the shapes of the clouds, the changing of colors and shapes. This person is enjoying the "form" of the sunset. If, on the other hand, the perception of the colours and shapes creates a context for the observer to reflect upon something of the human experience, such as humankind's minute position in the cosmos [or Shusterman suggests the potential of "a sunset experience involving complex interpretation or 'a sense of foreboding, insecurity, even of danger' (say, before some anticipated terrors in the night)"[22]], the conditions are ripe for an aesthetic experience. Thus, nature can provide aesthetic experiences, but more than perception of form is necessary if we are to experience nature (or works of art) aesthetically.

In arguing that more than "form" is required for an aesthetic response to occur, we must elaborate on what is entailed by aesthetic form and content. Although some aestheticians have tried to separate form and content and extol form as the aspect which gives art value [Clive Bell would be the most staunch proponent of this view], Sharon Bailin argues that form and content cannot be separated.

> Rather than being separate components which are simply added together to come up with a work, form and content are more like aspects of the same thing. The terms are abstractions which are helpful in discussing facets of works of art, but this need not imply that they are elements which can in reality be separated. . . . Any attempt to extract a content and express it in another form is necessarily inadequate since it will no longer be the same content. Similarly, there cannot be form in isolation. A form must be a form of something, and it is difficult to imagine how one could isolate the form of a work in order to attend to it alone.[23]

Acknowledging the importance of content *and* form is important in dealing with the criticism concerning the suggestion that the sunset example opens up too many experiences as being potentially "aesthetic" in nature. For example, someone could counter that contemplating a hair falling from his or her head could be a context for thinking about life and death. However, one could argue that a hair falling from one's head does not have a particular emphasis on form, that is, "how" the hair falls or what the hair looks like is not essential for provoking thoughts of life and death. This is not the case with the sunset. It is the sunset which fills the entire sky with intense colors and shapes which seem to lend itself to reflection upon the immensity and intensity of nature and thus, perhaps, humankind's minuteness in comparison.

Having considered the possibility of aesthetic responses to nature, I return now to the artistic. A criticism that may be raised is that my advocating "art for meaning's sake" applies only to certain kinds of art, that is, representational art, particular art forms, and so forth. Christopher Cordner, among others, questions the possibility of "meaning" in nonrepresentational art. "It just seems mistaken, because too intellectualist, to hold that abstract paintings express a conception of life-issues. And how could a piece of music express a conception of poverty, or war, or loyalty, or death, or honor? Architecture, and possibly dance, also seem unfitted to express conceptions of life-issues."[24] I think Cordner is wrong. Part of the problem lies in his use of the term "life-issues." In fairness to Cordner, however, he has adopted this term from Best, whose position Cordner is criticizing. Best suggests that "any art form, properly so-called, must at least allow for the possibility of the expression of a conception of life-issues such as contemporary moral, social and political problems."[25] Rather than using the term "life-issues," which connotes particular issues, usually issues involving a negative aspect of the human experience such as poverty, violence, and so forth, the term "human experience" would be more appropriate. To suggest that all art expresses something of the human experience would allow for the expression of negative and positive aspects of the human experience, including humankind's appreciation of form. Regarding dance, I have argued elsewhere[26] that dancers may not always express particular issues through dance, but when they are moving for the sake of movement, they are expressing thoughts pertaining to the joy of pure movement. Conceiving of art as expressing something of the human experience would seem to *allow* for Cordner's description of what happens when one engages with portraits. Cordner suggests that "[t]he force of the portrait lies not in its presenting us with a face on which it then makes a comment or about which it then expresses a conception, but in the vividness and fullness with which it realizes or makes manifest certain life-values."[27] Are these "life-values" not part of the human experience? Thus, Cordner's example *supports* my proposition that artists are always expressing something of the human experience through their work.

Regarding various art forms, all art forms have the potential to be responded to aesthetically. Hugo Meynell compares and contrasts different art forms by first suggesting features common to all art forms and then considering how the emphasis varies according to the specific art form under discussion.

> Each type of art is a matter of *manipulation of a medium* (a) to provide a *structure* (b) which is a means to satisfaction through *exercise and enlargement of consciousness*. While representation is certainly not the only means by which such an end may be secured, it is at least characteristic of literature and the visual arts that they exercise and enlarge consciousness through representation (c); and that such representation is more deeply satisfying when it involves some kind of reference to what is of central importance in human life (d).[28]

Regarding the specific artistic forms of literature, Meynell specifies the features deemed to be valuable.

> When examining the criticism of novels, plays, and other works of literature, such works are deemed to be of value in proportion to (i) their illustration and demonstration of what is of central importance for human

life; (ii) the originality of their use of language and their treatment of plot, character, situation, and so on; (iii) their just representation of people, things and circumstances; and (iv) their overall unity in variety of substance and effect. It will be seen that these features correspond respectively to (d), (a), (c) and (b) above.[29]

Regarding works of visual art, Meynell suggests that they "are found to be of value in proportion to (as well, presumably, as their exploitation of their medium as such) (i) their enhancement of perception and imagination (often through representation); (ii) their emotional significance; (iii) their unity in variety–which correspond to (c), (d), and (b)."[30] Finally, regarding works of music, Meynell suggests that their value "is found to be a matter of (i) its exploitation of the medium of sound as such; (ii) the clarity and intensity of its depiction of emotion and mood; (iii) its unity in variety–which correspond to (a), (d) and (b)."[31]

While Meynell considers the art forms of literature, visual art and music, Geraldine Dimondstein performs a similar analysis but she includes dance in her discussion.

> Each art form has its own distinguishing characteristics, provides a unique image, and uses particular media. How, then, can we give the arts a sense of unity as well as recognize their distinctiveness? To do so is to consider them in their broadest context, as parameters of space-time-force through which the functions of the arts are expressed. As parameters, they may have various values, yet each in its own way is necessary in creating and determining the aesthetic effects of any particular form. They cannot, then, be conceived as technical elements, but as the connective tissue underlying the expression of ideas and feelings.[32]

Dimondstein gives examples of how the same feature is expressed in different art forms. "When we speak of an energetic line or a strong color relationship in painting, of tension between the volumes or contours in a sculpture, of the power of a movement in dance or the intensity of an image in poetry, we are expressing a sense of vitality."[33]

Although the preceding discussion gives the impression that there are agreed-upon aesthetic features common to all art forms, as I have argued elsewhere,[34] one must be careful not to jump to the conclusion that one can come to understand these features apart from the works of which they are constitutive. H. Redfern makes this point when she insists that "aesthetic concepts (that is, concepts functioning aesthetically) are not grasped intellectually and then applied over a variety of instances: appreciation of works even within the same art form requires judgment (in that sense which involves perception and thought in felt experience) *in each particular case.*"[35]

The notions of judgment and particularity of works of art raises a whole set of questions which I have not yet addressed and which arise from the postmodern perspective. Although an examination of postmodern aesthetics would require a separate book, I must acknowledge that the analytic tradition that I have been espousing has come under attack from the postmodern camp. I will examine and respond, albeit briefly, to a few of the issues raised by some prominent postmodern thinkers.

A fundamental tenet of most postmodern thought involves a suspicion of value judgments (which would, needless to say, include aesthetic judgments). Stuart Sim, in reference to Jacques Derrida's postmodern project, states that "he [Derrida] celebrates the right to non-toleration of explication, the right to resist and frustrate the rationalist, rule-bound procedures of standardly constituted academic philosophy and criticism. Avoidance of explication, judgement without specified, or even specifiable, criteria."[36] Although many parties in the postmodern camp advocate the avoidance of judgment (which, ironically, would appear to be a judgment call in itself), there are some political implications of such a move which may need to be considered before one embraces the postmodern position (or lack of position). A useful example illuminating the potential dangers of erasing judgments can be found in the realm of feminism. In Sim's words:

> Radical feminism can therefore regard any game-playing with logocentricity, which, given patriarchy's stranglehold on most discourses, effectively means *phallogocentricity*, with approval. Placing under erasure that which has never taken your wishes into account, and which views you as the necessarily inferior side of a loaded binary opposition into the bargain, must be a very satisfying manoevure to perform. The off-critical refusal to play the value-judgement game takes on a whole new political dimension under such circumstances. That would be the positive reading of deconstruction's meaning for feminism. Could it not also be said, however, that deconstruction amounts to a moving of the goalposts as far as feminism is concerned? Its message might be put as follows: "do not bother to seek for power because power is illusory." An entire historical campaign to combat *exclusion* from significant discourses, the critical included, is thereby rendered problematical.[37]

Another fundamental tenet of postmodernism which, upon reflection, is also problematical, concerns the rejection of the "metanarrative." Jean-Francois Lyotard defines postmodern as "incredulity towards metanarrative."[38] The whole area of aesthetic appreciation is viewed by some postmodernists as representing a "metanarrative" which has been "written" by white, Anglo-Saxon males. However, distinguishing between "narratives" and "metanarratives" is problematic. In Sim's words:

> Like Derridean erasure it [the narrative/metanarrative distinction] claims to cancel out metaphysical commitments–and with them all problems about foundations–but it could be argued that it is in reality more a case of bracketing, which temporarily suspends but never totally eliminates the commitments in question. Allow Lyotard to call life, or any other sequence you care to name, a narrative, and he will draw you along with him from that point onwards, because you have tacitly accepted the bracketing of alternative explanations: a carefully engineered radical lack of prejudice in Lyotard's favour. . . . If life is a narrative then it must have a language, and if it has a language then it can be deconstructed. In Lyotard's view narrative is acceptable, whereas metanarrative is not. Metanarrative is foundational and thus to be avoided. We are therefore to try to ensure that life's narrative, the individual, is set free from life's metanarrative, the systems that control the individual. Once they are defined and applied, the terms play off each other with ease, forcing reality to conform to their requirements.[39]

Thus, postmodernism appears to be beset with insurmountable problems. I would agree with Sim when he concludes that "[a]nti-aesthetics as practiced by Derrida, Lyotard and their followers is ultimately self-defeating since it problematises their own judgements no less than those of their opponents."[40] Although postmodern thought involves much more than I have been able to explicate here, we must now return to the central thesis of this chapter and examine sport and its relationship to aesthetic activity.

"Aesthetic" Sport

I will now examine some aspects of sport in an attempt to determine what it is about sport that tempts us to refer to such activity as aesthetic. Best makes some distinctions concerning sport which prove to be a good starting point. Best distinguishes between sports such as football, climbing, and track and field, which he calls "purposive," and sports such as synchronized swimming, trampolining, and gymnastics, which he refers to as "aesthetic."[41] Regarding purposive sports, Best states that "[i]n each of these sports the aim, purpose or end can be specified independently of the manner of achieving it as long as it conforms to the limits set by the rules or norms–for example, scoring a goal and climbing the Eiger."[42] [I will not get into Terence Roberts's decimation of Best's generalization of ends at this time, since for my purposes it suffices to distinguish sports where the aesthetic dimension is not fundamental (even though it exists in the particular) from sports where the aesthetic dimension *is* fundamental]. Although, according to Best, an aesthetic experience is unnecessary in the context of a purposive sport, he points out that it is possible to experience aesthetic feelings while participating in such sports. He cites examples such as

a finely timed stroke in squash, a smoothly accomplished series of movements in gymnastics, an outing in an "eight" when the whole crew is pulling in unison, with unwavering balance, and a training run when one's body seems to be completely under one's control. For many, the feelings derived from such performances are part of the enjoyment of participation, and "aesthetic" seems the most appropriate way to characterise them.[43]

The feelings described by Best should not be referred to as aesthetic. Although they may satisfy the "sensuous" condition for sensuous understanding (in perhaps both the "feeling" and "sense" dimensions), there is no deeper understanding of an expressed aspect of the human experience attained in these situations. It is important at this point to emphasize the notion of an "expressed aspect" of the human experience. Participating in sporting activity *is* part of the human experience. However, there is an important difference between *participating* in a human experience and *expressing* an aspect of that experience. An example from the realm of art will help illuminate this distinction. Jerrold Levinson cites the example of a controversial art piece displayed on his campus, which he calls *Rape Piece.*[44] *Rape Piece* consisted of a wall erected to display the names of all the male students listed in the campus directory. At the head of this giant poster was the rubric "Potential Rapists." On the surface, this poster looked like a public notice (similar to a "Wanted" poster). If this were the case, the poster would be part of the human experience, that is, an attempt to track down suspected rapists. However, that was not the intention of the artists. In Levinson's words:

> *Rape Piece* is not strictly an item of that category [public notice category], it only resembles such; what it is, at base, is an artistic representation of such an item. That is to say, the creators of *Rape Piece* have borrowed the form of a public proclamation of warning and used it in an image–an image, however, which is knowingly indiscernible from the thing itself, at least if intention and framing context are ignored or left out of account.[45]

The importance of "intention and framing context" is evident in the aesthetic realm but not in the sporting realm. The sports person is participating in a human experience but he or she is not intending to express some aspect of that experience by his or her participation in the sport. The experiencing and the expression of an experience is a distinction of fundamental importance when comparing and contrasting sport and aesthetic activities.

By suggesting that the term "aesthetic" not be used to label the feelings involved in sport, that is, Best's "finely tuned stroke, smoothly accomplished series of movements," and so forth, I am not denying their existence nor their significance. In fact, these feelings are critical for the satisfaction one derives from participation in sport. However, I would adopt the notion of "flow," which the psychologist Mihaly Czikszentmihalyi has coined, as a better descriptor than "aesthetic" in describing the feelings Best is referring to. Czikszentmihalyi, after interviewing hundreds of people pursuing activities such as rock-climbing, basketball and dancing in an attempt to discover what it was about these activities which were perceived as rewarding, found that a majority of these people reported similar experiential states. He described this state in the following manner. "He [participant interviewed] experiences it [the 'flow' state] as a unified flowing from one moment to the next, in which he is in control of his actions, and in which there is little distinction between self and environment, between stimulus and response, or between past, present, and future."[46] This "flow" state seems to be what E. F. Kaelin is referring to in his discussion of aesthetic perception in sport when he states that "[t]he feeling of being at one with nature, using it to fulfill our own aims with consummate ease, is a direct aesthetic response of the mover to his motion"[47] and Kupfer in his suggestion that "[c]oncepts such as timing, jelling, flowing, harmonizing, and executing attest to this aesthetic ideal in competitive sport."[48] Once again, I would propose using "flow" rather than "aesthetic" to describe this response.

Regarding the sports Best refers to as "aesthetic sports," for example, gymnastics and diving, their purpose cannot be considered apart from the manner of achieving it. Best cites the example of vaulting in gymnastics: "The end is not simply to get over the box somehow or other, even if one were to do so in a clumsy way and collapse afterwards in an uncontrolled manner. The way in which the appropriate movements are performed is not incidental but central to such a sport."[50] It is perhaps the aesthetic sport experience which has led many theorists to make a connection between aesthetics and sports. However, once again, the concept of "aesthetic" has been misapplied to these sports. At this point, I must note that Best *does* make a distinction between sport and art.[51] However, I want to push this distinction further and propose that sport differs not only from art, but also from the more general experience we refer to as aesthetic. In conceiving of the aesthetic as "sensuous understanding," it is important to reiterate the condition of attaining an understanding of the human experience. This does not happen in sport, not even aesthetic sports. I am not denying the fundamental role that "form" plays in aesthetic sports. However, aesthetic experience involves not only the apprehension of form, but also content. It is how the content of a work of art, for instance, is expressed, which makes a richer understanding of that content possible. Since the content necessary for an aesthetic experience is lacking in aesthetic sports, the term "form sports" would be a more appropriate epithet for these sports.

If we consider various sports to lie on a continuum (a hierarchy would be more appropriate but I want to avoid the impression that some sports/activities are more valuable than others), we could place "flow" sports at one end and "aesthetic" activity at the other. In between these ends, we would have "form" sports. Now, starting at the "flow" end, we would be adding particular aspects as we moved to the "aesthetic" end. In other words, all sports and aesthetic activity have the potential for the participants in these activities to achieve a state of "flow." As we move along the continuum to the "form" sports, we add an emphasis on form, that is, on "how" certain movements are performed. When we arrive at the "aesthetic" end, where I would place dance forms such as creative and modern, we no longer have only the possibility of achieving a "flow" state and an emphasis on "form," but also the added dimension of expressing some aspect of the human experience. Regarding dance forms such as folk and jazz dance, they lie somewhere between form sports and aesthetic activity. In other words, some folk and jazz dance do express some aspects of the human experience, but often these dances are more a series of movements with an emphasis on form, that is, particular steps.

In suggesting that an aesthetic experience involves the expression of some content, I have to deal with a counter-example that is evident in the work of Kaelin and Kupfer. Kaelin suggests that aesthetic expression is evident when "[t]he tempo and rhythm of the game are defined in terms of the building up and the release of dynamic tensions, created ultimately by the opposition of equally capable teams."[52] Kupfer suggests that "[t]he interdependence of team members contesting the opposition yields tensions and resolutions which echo those arising from the circumstances in which real people are situated."[53] What can be read into these descriptions is that sport competitions express the concept of tension between players. How would this differ from a dance piece that expressed tension between humans, or humans and their environment? The difference lies in the intention of the experience. In an activity whose fundamental purpose is an aesthetic one, that is, the creation of a dance piece, the expression of tension between humans, or humans and their environment would be the sole purpose of that activity. On the other hand, in a sporting context, the tension between players is a by-product of the design of the game. The expression of this tension is not the fundamental purpose of sport. In fact, there are many sports where such overt tension is not evident, for example, individuals sports such as diving. The critic could respond by suggesting that in the case of diving, the tension is between the diver and the standards of the dive he or she is attempting to perform. However, such a perception is stretching the notion of tension.

A similar counter-example is found in the work of J. M. Boxill, who proposes that sports *are* concerned with life situations and that sport performances exhibit this aesthetically. This concern is made in response to Best's argument that art, *not* sport, deals with life-issues. Boxill cites the examples of the widening of the 3-second lane in basketball to prevent success without hard work being an expression of the idea of success through effort, and the evolving of the New Games being an expression of the dangers of competition.[54] In a vein similar to my response to Kaelin's and Kupfer's suggestions that sports express the life situation of tension, if anything similar to the expression of a life situation *is* being expressed, it is purely a by-product of the design of the game. In Boxill's examples, her interpretation of the situations is even more tenuous than the notion of games expressing tension. The widening of the 3-second lane in basketball could just as easily be explained by looking at what it means to design a game, that is, imposing limitations to present a challenge, and, realizing that more of a challenge was needed in the game of basketball, a change was made to the 3-second lane. Regarding the New Games, rather than being viewed as a social commentary on the dangers of competition, they could just as easily be viewed as another form of games which presents an alternative to people who prefer non-competitive games, sometimes exclusive from, but sometimes in addition to, competitive games. Thus, sport is not concerned with "life-issues" in the same intentional way that aesthetic activity is concerned with expressing facets of the human experience.

A more damaging criticism to my thesis that aesthetic activity, not sport, is primarily concerned with the expression of thoughts, feelings, ideas, which evoke an enriched understanding of the human condition, is the proposal that humankind expresses meaning through sport. Kretchmar suggests that "games send messages" such as "success is good," "freedom (opportunity) is good" and "justice is good."[55] Once again, however, the sending of these "messages" is not the intention of the sports player. They may be a by-product, but they are not the reason people play sport. However, the sending and receiving of "messages" is an important reason why people engage in aesthetic activity, either as artists or appreciators of art (or appreciators of nature, for that matter). I must emphasize that sport is a meaningful activity, but there is an important distinction between engaging in a meaningful activity and expressing the meaning in an activity. A good example would be a dance dealing with the physical tension involved in a sport such as football. A football player could play a game of football and experience physical tension. The dancer, however, attempts to express the meaning of physical tension by creating movements which may resemble moves in a football game, but the purpose of these movements are not to score a touchdown, but rather to express the meaning of physical tension. The importance of the distinction between experiencing and expressing an aspect of the human experience cannot be overemphasized.   Although removing the label "aesthetic" from the realm of sports may appear to be devaluing sport to some degree, I would argue on the contrary. The potential for "flow" feelings and focus on "form" are still being acknowledged. However, although "flow" and "form" sport are important, they should not be considered aesthetic. Activities such as creative or modern dance truly deserves the denotation "aesthetic" since the purpose of these dance forms is to express ideas, feelings and thoughts through movement.   This expression is an attempt to achieve a sensuous understanding, both on the part of the dancer and the audience. The attainment of a sensuous understanding is what it means to have an aesthetic experience. Thus a physical education program must have a heavy emphasis on creative and modern dance, not only sport, if it is to involve expressive as well as functional aspects of human movement.

Conclusion

The purpose of *Socrates, Sport, and Students* was to provide a philosophical justification for the inclusion of physical education in the school system. Because this justification ushered in a number of related topics, I will summarize the main argument and how it connected with the other topics discussed in the book. Then I will conclude with some suggestions for further research in an effort to improve the physical education experience for future students.

The justificatory argument for physical education proposed in this book was based on the possibility of acquiring practical knowledge through participation in physical activities. Carr outlined conditions for assessing practical knowledge which parallel the "justified, true belief" conditions for assessing theoretical knowledge; that is, for one to know how to do x, one must 1) entertain $x$ing as a purpose, 2) be acquainted with a set of practical procedures for successful $x$ing, and 3) exhibit recognizable success at $x$ing.

Before examining more closely the conditions for assessing practical knowledge, a justification for an education having anything to do with "knowledge" is required. I argued that knowledge is constitutive of the pursuit of rationality and that the pursuit of rationality is intrinsically justifiable as the prime educational aim. Although philosophers of education have proposed other educational aims, the debate over educational aims cannot even "get off the ground" without relying on rational thought, that is, the giving of reasons (in this case, reasons for choosing one educational aim over another).

Returning to the conditions for assessing practical knowledge, the first condition of entertaining $x$ing as a purpose, has to do with the notion of intentionality; that is, activities making up the physical education curriculum are activities which have the potential to be learned. We would not call a "beginner's luck" situation, for example, hitting a target on the first try, a learned situation. So, even if a student experienced such "luck," we would not want to say he or she "knew" how to perform the activity under consideration.

The second condition of assessing practical knowledge, that is, being acquainted with a set of practical procedures for successful *x*ing, is closely related to the conception of critical thinking described by Siegel who viewed a critical thinker as one who is "appropriately moved by reasons." The necessary and sufficient conditions for someone to be classified a critical thinker include both being skilled at reason assessment and having a critical spirit. The critical spirit and the underlying epistemology concerned with the giving of reasons are generalizable. However, there is a connection between critical thinking and subject-specific content knowledge and this connection is important for justifying the teaching of critical thinking in physical education. The teaching of critical thinking can be justified in that students should be helped to develop skills and dispositions with which they can exercise sound judgments and take control of their lives. This respect for the autonomy of students as persons is a powerful justification for teaching critical thinking. Specifically in a physical education context, critical thinking can be justified as being important in developing practical knowledge in that both being acquainted with a set of practical procedures for successful *x*ing and exhibiting recognizable success at *x*ing require critical thinking.

The third condition for assessing practical knowledge, that is, exhibiting recognizable success at xing, involves critical thinking in the sense that critical thinking is involved in moral reasoning. The development of moral reasoning is an important part of moral education, and moral education is logically connected to physical education as a result of the third condition for assessing practical knowledge. If students are to exhibit recognizable success at *x*ing, they must have something with which they can compare their skills and abilities. Competitive activities are an important factor in this comparison process. In responding to educators who view competition as a negative thing, a distinction had to be made between positive and negative results as a consequence of participating in competitive activities and the view that competition is intrinsically positive or negative. When examining and critiquing the notion that competition is intrinsically positive or negative, it is helpful to consider the root word of competition, *com-petitio*, meaning "to strive together." The proposition that competition is intrinsically selfish cannot withstand an analysis of what is meant by "selfish." Competition is intrinsically positive, and furthermore, participation in competitive activities provides the opportunity to develop skills in the pursuit of excellence. Thus, competition should not be discouraged in physical education classes.

The competitive situation that I am advocating is one that involves a respect for mutually agreed upon rules as well as a respect for opponents as persons. This respect for rules and opponents is not always evident in competitive situations and if we are to achieve *competitio*, a significant component of the physical education program must be concerned with moral education. Moral education can take a number of forms and teaching by example and by precept are both necessary for students to acquire the moral reasoning required for *competitio* to be realized.

Whether athletes do reason morally in specific situations is more of an empirical rather than philosophical question. However, I interviewed university level athletes to ascertain the kind of ethical issues they faced and how they resolved them. In analyzing the reasons the athletes gave in resolving the ethical issues they faced, I distinguished six categories of reasons–reasons concerned with 1) "doing unto others as you would have them do unto you," 2) fairness, 3) respecting others, 4) not hurting the team, 5) respect for the game, and 6) fear of getting caught. These reasons were interpreted using moral philosophy, focusing on the moral theories of Kantianism, virtue theory, and ethical egoism. The fact that the hockey players interviewed could not think of any ethical issues in their sport opened up the whole area of whether sport experiences should be subjected to the same moral considerations as other life experiences. If an affirmative answer is arrived at, then the possibility of providing an education in the area of moral reasoning becomes tenable. This possibility leads to the second area where the interviews with the athletes were informative; that is, reviewing the categories of reasons cited and their reflection of moral theory can help teachers and coaches facilitate the development of moral reasoning skills in their students and athletes. Finally, the very possibility of the athletes articulating the reasons they have for making certain ethical decisions has implications for how teachers and coaches can help facilitate the development of moral reasoning.

The influence of the coaches on their athletes was a recurring theme with the athletes interviewed. Thus, I interviewed the coaches, asking questions similar to those asked of the athletes, with the exception of also asking the coaches how much autonomy they thought athletes should have. I also conducted a philosophical analysis of the concept of "autonomy". When autonomy is understood as "self-sufficiency," it is no wonder that some coaches viewed the granting of autonomy to their athletes as fatal to the athletic enterprise. However, if autonomy is understood as "self-rule," with the athlete acting as "helmsperson," the coach would then play a fundamental role as "information provider." The analogous situation of "informed consent" in medicine allowed for a large degree of input from the coach while still respecting the autonomy of the athlete. This situation assumed that the coach has the requisite knowledge to be *an* authority regarding the sport he or she coaches, rather than just being *in* a position of authority. Thus, if a coach who is an authority sought informed consent from his or her athletes, then athletes would find themselves in a position where they could grow, not only as athletes, but as autonomous individuals.

The issue of autonomy and athletes raised the question of the relationship between coaching and teaching. When sport involves the acquisition of practical knowledge, the coach plays the role of teacher. Rather than supporting the training/educating dichotomy with the coach perceived as trainer and the teacher as educator, I suggested that the coach should expand his or her perspective to move beyond the narrow focus of physical skill acquisition to include the affective and cognitive domains. As in the case of an educator, the coach should also view his or her task as connecting with a wider set of beliefs, that is, ethical as well as metaphysical beliefs. Finally, the coach should adopt the educational ideal of helping his or her athletes develop as autonomous individuals.

As well as the above mentioned commonalities between teaching and coaching, there are some contrasts–these having to do with the function of sport and physical education in our society. Sport cannot be solely identified as being educational. There are contexts where sport is more concerned with instrumental functions, that is, the experience of fun or the acquisition of money. Just as sport cannot be equated solely with physical education, physical education cannot involve only sport. Human movement involves both functional and expressive movements and sport, even "aesthetic sport," does not fulfill the expressive aspects of human movement. Thus a distinction has to be made between "aesthetic sports" and activities, such as dance, which are truly expressive.

Thus, I conclude my philosophical analysis into physical education and sport. The book began with a justification for the inclusion of physical education in the educational curriculum. However, a justification based on the acquisition of practical knowledge quickly ushered in the topics of critical thinking, competition, moral education, the relationship between coaches and athletes, and the relationship between physical education and sport. I hope I have done justice to these topics. It is also my hope that physical educators will take seriously their role as "educators," in the sense of facilitating the acquisition of knowledge–both theoretical and practical–in their students. This role includes not only the modeling of physical skills, but also the disposition and spirit of critical thinking and moral reasoning. With an emphasis on acquiring practical skills, critical thinking and moral reasoning, physical educators can help students develop into physically skilled and autonomous people.

Although *Socrates, Sport, and Students* is a philosophical inquiry, the issues raised in the book could stimulate empirical research. For example, if physical educators focused on the developing of practical knowledge, students could be tested on their ability to perform whatever skills were being taught. Whether an emphasis on critical thinking made a difference could be tested by having a research group engage in activities which involve critical thinking, for example, having students analyze movements in order to provide reasons for why one approach would be more effective than another, and then having this group compare their practical knowledge of specific skills with students in a control group which did not focus on critical thinking activities. Whether competitive situations helped students improve their skill level could also be tested, with a control group practicing skills in non-competitive situations while the research group competed with opponents, records, times, and so forth. The skill levels of participants in each group could be tested to assess the effects of competitive situations. The role of moral education in the physical education context could be studied by observing the behaviour of students whose teacher emphasized respecting opponents and rules and comparing the behaviour with a class where moral education was not emphasized. As well as observing overt behaviour, students could be questioned as to why they did or did not behave in a certain manner, in order to ascertain their moral reasoning ability. The above research projects are only a few possible options but they do suggest ways of testing the ideas in this book–ideas which form an argument to justify physical education in the educational curriculum as well as, hopefully, improve the physical education programs experienced by students.

Endnotes

Chapter 1

1. R. Scott Kretchmar, *Practical Philosophy of Sport* (Champaign, Illinois: Human Kinetics, 1994), 150.

2. Jim Parry, "Physical Education, Justification and the National Curriculum," *Physical Education Review* 11 (1988): 106-18, 110.

3. Ibid.

4. Ibid.

5. Ibid., 111.

6. In a recent publication (*European Physical Education Review* 3, no. 2 [1997]), David Carr expresses a lack of confidence in his earlier argument. Although he now doubts the educational (but not necessarily, schooling) value of hockey or volleyball, he has left the issue "to the future reflections of interested professionals" (203). Since Carr admits that he has "not much idea what to say about hockey or volleyball" (203), I would continue to advocate his earlier argument until a convincing counter-argument *is* put forth.

7. R. S. Peters, *Ethics and Education* (London: George Allen and Unwin, 1966), 26.

8. Ibid., 165.

9. Harvey Siegel, *Educating Reason: Rationality, Critical Thinking, and Education.* New York: Routledge, 1988), 32.

10. R. S. Peters, "Education as Initiation," in *Philosophical Analysis and Education,* ed. R. Archambault (New York: Humanities Press, 1965), 104.

11. Ibid., 103.

12. David Carr, "Aims of Physical Education," *Physical Education Review* 2 (1979): 91-100.

13. Ibid., 95.

14. Peters, "Education as Initiation," 103.

15. Paul H. Hirst, *Knowledge and the Curriculum* (London: Routledge and Kegan Paul, 1974), 28.

16. Paul H. Hirst, "Education, Knowledge and Practices," in *Beyond Liberal Education: Essays in Honour of Paul H. Hirst,* eds. Robin Barrow and Patricia White (London: Routledge, 1993), 197.

17. Aristotle *Nicomachean Ethics* 1140a 33 – 1140b 6.

18. G. E. M. Anscombe, *Intention* (Oxford: Basil Blackwell, 1957), 88.

19. Gilbert Ryle, *The Concept of Mind* (London: Hutchinson, 1949), 28.

20. Ibid., 32.

21. David Carr, "Practical Reasoning and Knowing How," *Journal of Human Movement Studies* 4 (1978): 3-20.

22. Stuart Hampshire, *Thought and Action* (London: Chatto and Windus, 1959), 131.

23. Ibid., 78.

24. Saul Ross, *Persons, Minds and Bodies: A Transcultural Dialogue Amongst Physical Education, Philosophy and the Social Sciences* (North York, Ontario: University of Toronto Press, 1988), 24.

25. Ibid.

26. Ibid.

27. Hampshire, *Thought and Action*, 167.

28. To avoid the consequence that using Carr's conditions for assessing practical knowledge could also justify learning how to engage in the "practical" activities of stealing and torturing (a point brought to my attention by Dr. Murray Elliot), I propose adding a fourth condition referring to moral acceptability of the knowledge being acquired.

29. David Carr, "Knowledge in Practice," *American Philosophical Quarterly* 18 (1981): 53-61, 59.

30. Ibid.

31. Ibid.

32. Ibid., 60.

33. Ibid.

34. Peter J. Arnold, "The Preeminence of Skill as an Educational Value in the Movement Curriculum," *Quest* 43 (1991): 66-77, 69.

35. Fred L. Martens, *Basic Concepts of Physical Education: The Foundations in Canada* (Champaign, Illinois: Stipes Publishing Company, 1986), 94.

36. Derek C. Meakin, "How Physical Education can Contribute to Personal and Social Education," *Physical Education Review* 2 (1990): 108-19, 115.

37. Ibid., 118

38. Cornel M. Hamm, *Philosophical Issues in Education: An Introduction* (New York: The Falmer Press, 1989), 30-31.

Chapter 2

1. Paul H. Hirst, "Education, Knowledge and Practices," in *Beyond Liberal Education: Essays in Honour of Paul H. Hirst*, ed. Robin Barrow and Patricia White (London: Routledge, 1993), 187.

2. Jim Parry, "Physical Education, Justification and the National Curriculum," *Physical Education Review* 11 (1988): 106-18, 111.

3. John White, *The Aims of Education Restated* (London: Routledge and Kegan Paul, 1982), 10.

4. Paul H. Hirst, "Liberal Education and the Nature of Knowledge," in *The Philosophy of Education*, ed. R. S. Peters (Oxford: Oxford University Press, 1973), 100.

5. White, *The Aims of Education Restated*, 10.

6. Ibid.

7. R. S. Downie, Eileen M. Loudfoot and Elizabeth Telfer, *Education and Personal Relationships* (London: Methuen and Co., 1974), 50.

8. Ibid.

9. White, *The Aims of Education Restated*, 11.

10. Aladair C. MacIntyre, "Against Utilitarianism," in *Aims in Education: The Philosophic Approach*, ed. T. H. B. Hollins (Manchester: Manchester University Press, 1964), 19.

11. White, *The Aims of Education Restated*, 15.

12. Ibid., 16.

13. Ibid., 10.

14. Ibid.

15. I am grateful to Dr. Eamonn Callan for setting me straight on the distinction between constitutive and instrumental.

16. MacIntyre, "Against Utilitarianism," 19.

17. White, *The Aims of Education Restated*, 16.

18. Andrew Reid, "Value Pluralism and Physical Education," *European Physical Education Review* 3 (1997): 6-20, 8-9.

19. Ibid., 10.

20. Ibid.

21. White, *The Aims of Education Restated*, 23.

22. Ibid., 58.

23. Donald Arnstine, "The Educator's Impossible Dream: Knowledge as an Educational Aim," in *Philosophy of Education 1992*, ed. H. A. Alexander (Urbana, Illinois: Philosophy of Education Society, 1992), 261.

24. Ibid.

25. Reid, "Value Pluralism," 9.

26. Hirst, "Education, Knowledge and Practices," 184.

27. Ibid., 190.

28. Ibid., 191.

29. Ibid., p. 197.

30. Kevin Williams, "On Learning for its Own Sake," *Prospero* 3 (1997): 10-13, 12.

31. R. S. Peters, "What is an Educational Process?" in *The Concept of Education*, ed. R. S. Peters (London: Routledge and Kegan Paul, 1967), 19.

32. Hirst, "Education, Knowledge and Practices," 197.

33. C. J. B. Macmillan, "Love and Logic in 1984," in *Philosophy of Education 1984*, ed. Emily E. Robertson (Illinois State University: Philosophy of Education society, 1984), 11.

34. Sheryle Bergmann Drewe, "The Rational Underpinning of Aesthetic Experience: Implications for Arts Education," *Canadian Review of Art* 26 (1999): 22-33.

35. John Colbeck, "Against Reason," *Revista espanola de pedagogia* ano L (1992): 515-25, 520.

36. Harvey Siegel, *Educating Reason: Rationality, Critical Thinking, and Education* (New York: Routledge, 1988), 32.

37. Harvey Siegel, *Rationality Redeemed? Further Dialogues on an Educational Ideal* (New York: Routledge, 1997), 4.

38. Ibid., 102.

39. Nicholas Burbules, "Reasonable Doubt: Toward a Postmodern Defense of Reason as an Educational Aim," in *Critical Conversations in Philosophy of Education*, ed. Wendy Kohli (New York: Routledge, 1995), 96.

40. Siegel, *Rationality Redeemed?*, 110.

41. R. Rorty, "Solidarity or Objectivity?" in *Relativism: Interpretation and Confrontation*, ed. M. Krauz (Notre Dame: University of Notre Dame Press, 1989), 35-50, 36, 44, quoted in H. Siegel, "On Some Recent Challenges to the Ideal of Reason," *Inquiry: Critical Thinking Across the Disciplines* 15 (1996): 2-16, 8.

42. Harvey Siegel, "On Some Recent Challenges to the Ideal of Reason," *Inquiry: Critical Thinking Across the Disciplines* 15 (1996): 2-16, 9.

43. Ibid.

44. Ibid., 7.

45. Ibid., 13.

46. Peter Abbs, "Introduction" in *The Symbolic Order: A Contemporary Reader on the Arts Debate*, ed. P. Abbs (London: Falmer Press, 1989), 1.

Chapter 3

1. Richard Paul, "Understanding Substantive Critical Thinking: Avoiding the Growing List of Counterfeits," in *Critical Thinking: Events and Resources for College and University Educators* (Santa Rosa, CA: The Center and Foundation for Critical Thinking, Spring 1995), 11.

2. Ralph Johnson, "The Problem of Defining Critical Thinking," in *The Generalizability of Critical Thinking: Multiple Perspectives on an Educational Ideal*, ed. Stephen P. Norris (New York: Teachers College Press, 1992), 53.

3. Robert H. Ennis, "A Concept of Critical Thinking," *Harvard Educational Review* 32 (1962): 81-111, 83-84.

4. Robert H. Ennis, "A Taxonomy of Critical Thinking Dispositions and Abilities," in *Teaching Thinking Skills: Theory and Practice*, ed. Joan Boykoff Baron and Robert J. Sternberg (New York: W. H. Freeman, 1987), 10-15.

5. Richard Paul, *Critical Thinking: What Every Person Needs to Survive in a Rapidly Changing World*, 3rd ed., rev. (Santa Rosa, CA: Foundation for Critical Thinking, 1993), 138.

6. Richard Paul, "Teaching Critical Thinking in the 'Strong' Sense: A Focus on Self-Deception, World Views, and a Dialectical Mode of Analysis," *Informal Logic Newsletter* 4 (1982): 2-7, 3.

7. Harvey Siegel, *Educating Reason: Rationality, Critical Thinking, and Education.* New York: Routledge, 1988), 17.

8. Paul, *Critical Thinking*, 137.

9. Matthew Lipman, *Thinking in Education* (Cambridge: Cambridge University Press, 1991), 116.

10. Ibid., 117-23.

11. Paul, *Critical Thinking*, 136.

12. Matthew Lipman, "Good Thinking," *Inquiry: Critical Thinking Across the Disciplines* 15 (1995): 37-41, 37.

13. Johnson, "The Problem of Defining Critical Thinking," 46.

14. Siegel, *Educating Reason*, 34.

15. Ibid., 41, 32.

16. See Barbara J. Thayer-Bacon, "Caring and its Relationship to Critical Thinking," *Educational Theory* 43 (1993): 323-40, 329.

17. Siegel, *Educating Reason*, 32.

18. Sheryle Bergmann, "An Analysis of the Feminist Critique of the Claims that the Prime Aim of Education is to Develop Critical Thinking," *The Journal of Educational Thought* 28 (1994): 165-78.

19. John E. McPeck, *Critical Thinking and Education* (New York: St. Martin's Press, 1981), 4.

20. Siegel, *Educating Reason*, 19.

21. Paul, *Critical Thinking*, 364.

22. Siegel, *Educating Reason*, 32.

23. Ennis, "A Taxonomy of Critical Thinking," 10.

24. Paul, *Critical Thinking*, 138.

25. Lipman, *Thinking in Education*, 116.

26. McPeck, *Critical Thinking*, 9.

27. Robert H. Ennis, "The Degree to which Critical Thinking is Subject Specific: Clarification and Needed Research," in *The Generalizability of Critical Thinking: Multiple Perspectives on an Educational Ideal*, ed. Stephen P. Norris (New York: Teachers College Press, 1992), 22-23.

28. See Fran Cleland and Cynthia Pearse, "Critical Thinking in Elementary Physical Education: Reflections on a Year Long Study," *Journal of Physical Education, Recreation and Dance* 66 (1995): 31-38; Karen M. Greenockle and Gracie J. Purvis, "Redesigning a Secondary School Wellness Unit Using the Critical Thinking Model," *Journal of Physical Education, Recreation, and Dance* 66 (1995): 49-52; Ron E. McBride, "Critical Thinking–An Overview with Implications for Physical Education," *Journal of Teaching in Physical Education* 11 (1991): 112-25; Susan Schwager and Cathy Labate, "Teaching for Critical Thinking in Physical Education," *Journal of Physical Education, Recreation and Dance* 64 (1993): 24-26; and Shari Tishman and David N.

Perkins, "Critical Thinking and Physical Education," *Journal of Physical Education, Recreation, and Dance* 66 (1995): 24-30.

29. Immanuel Kant, *Foundations of the Metaphysics of Morals*, trans. Lewis White Beck (New York: Bobbs-Merrill, 1959), 47.

30. Ibid., 54.

31. Siegel, *Educating Reason*, 56.

32. Ennis, "A Taxonomy of Critical Thinking," 10-15.

33. Siegel, *Educating Reason*, 57.

34. Ibid., 58.

35. David Carr, "Knowledge in Practice," *American Philosophical Quarterly* 18 (1981): 53-61.

36. Cleland and Pearse, "Critical Thinking in Elementary Physical Education," 36-37.

37. See Glenn Kirchner, *Physical Education for Elementary School Children*, 8th ed. (Dubuque, IA: Wm. C. Brown Publishers, 1992); Beverly Nichols, *Moving and Learning: The Elementary School Physical Education Experience*, 3rd ed. (St. Louis: Mosby, 1994);   and Robert P. Pangrazi and Victor P. Dauer, *Dynamic Physical Education for Elementary School Children*, 10th ed. (New York: Macmillan Publishing Co., 1992).

38. Robert M. Hautala, "Enhancing Games Through Critical Thinking," *Teaching Elementary Physical Education* 2 (1991): 8-9.

39. Cleland and Pearse, "Critical Thinking in Elementary Physical Education," 37.

40. Schwager and Labate, "Teaching for Critical Thinking," 25.

41. Peter J. Arnold, "Education, Movement, and the Rationality of Practical Knowledge," *Quest* 40 (1988): 115-25.

42. Cleland and Pearse, "Critical Thinking in Elementary Physical Education," 37.

43. Greenockle and Purvis, "Redesigning a Secondary School Wellness Unit," 49.

44. Ibid., 50.

45. Tishman and Perkins, "Critical Thinking and Physical Education," 28.

Chapter 4

1. Eleanor Metheny, *Vital Issues* (Washington, DC: American Alliance for Health, Physical Education, and Recreation, 1977), 71.

2. Terry Orlick, *Winning Through Cooperation: Competitive Insanity, Cooperative Alternatives* (Washington, DC: Acropolis Books, 1978).

3. Metheny, *Vital Issues*, 71.

4. Drew A. Hyland, "Competition and Friendship," in *Philosophic Inquiry in Sport*, ed. William J. Morgan and Klaus V. Meier, 1ˢᵗ ed. (Champaign, IL: Human Kinetics, 1988), 236.

5. Robert L. Simon, *Fair Play: Sports, Values, and Society* (Boulder, CO: Westview Press, 1991), 23.

6. Ibid., 28.

7. Hollis F. Fait and John E. Billing, "Reassessment of the Value of Competition," in *Joy and Sadness in Children's Sports*, ed. Rainer Martens (Champaign, IL: Human Kinetics, 1978), 101.

8. This point was brought to my attention by Dr. Dan Bailis.

9. David N. Campbell, "On Being Number One: Competition in Education," *Phi Delta Kappan* 56 (1974): 143-46, 145.

10. Steve Grineski, "Children, Cooperative Learning, and Physical Education," *Teaching Elementary Physical Education* 4 (1993): 10-14, 11.

11. See M. Fielding, "Against Competition," in *Proceedings of the Philosophy of Education Society of Great Britain* 10 (1976): 124-146; Alfie Kohn, *No Contest: The Case Against Competition* (Boston: Houghton Mifflin Company, 1986); and John H. Schaar, "Equality of Opportunity and Beyond," in *Equality, Nomos* 9, ed. J. Roland Pennock and John W. Chapman (New York: Atherton Press, 1967).

12. Kohn, *No Contest*, 116.

13. Fielding, "Against Competition," 140.

14. Simon, *Fair Play*, 20.

15. Jay J. Coakley, *Sport in Society: Issues and Controversies*, 5th ed. (St. Louis, MO: Mosby, 1994), 94.

16. Ibid., 100.

17. Charles Bailey, "Games, Winning and Education," *Cambridge Journal of Education* 5 (1975): 40-50, 45.

18. Fait and Billing, "Reassessment of the Value of Competition," 101.

19. Ronald Dworkin, *Taking Rights Seriously* (Cambridge, MA: Harvard University Press, 1977), 227.

20. Simon, *Fair Play*, 30.

21. Hyland, "Competition and Friendship," 236.

22. John R. Searle, *The Construction of Social Reality* (New York: The Free Press, 1995), 27-8.

23. Peter J. Arnold, "Education, Movement, and the Rationality of Practical Knowledge," *Quest* 40 (1988): 115-25, 60.

24. Francis Dunlop, "Bailey on Games, Winning and Education," *Cambridge Journal of Education* 5 (1975): 153-160, 159.

25. Simon, *Fair Play*, 28.

26. Ibid.

27. L. Perry, "Competition and Cooperation," *British Journal of Educational Studies* 23 (1975): 127-34, 128.

28. Leon Festinger, "A Theory of Social Comparison Processes," *Human Relations* 7 (1954): 117-40, 117-20.

29. See Stephen Dakin and A. John Arrowood, "The Social Comparison of Ability," *Human Relations* 34 (1981): 89-109; John Gastorf, Jerry Suls, and John Lawhon, "Opponent Choices of Below Average Performers," *Bulletin of*

the *Psychonomic Society* 12 (1978): 217-20; and Jerry M. Suls and R. L. Miller, eds., *Social Comparison Processes: Theoretical and Empirical Perspectives* (Washington, DC: Hemisphere, 1977).

30. Carolyn Thomas, *Sport in a Philosophic Context* (Philadelphia: Lea and Febiger, 1983), 78.

31. Peter McIntosh, *Fair Play: Ethics in Sport and Education.* London: Heinemann, 1979), 178.

32. James W. Keating, "The Ethics of Competition and its Relation to Some Moral Problems in Athletics," in *The Philosophy of Sport: A Collection of Original Essays*, ed. Robert G. Osterhoudt (Springfield, IL: Thomas, 1973), 159.

33. Alice E. Kildea, "Competition: A Model for Conception," *Quest* 35 (1983): 169-81.

34. Simon, *Fair Play*, 23.

35. Paul Weiss, *Sport: A Philosophic Inquiry* (Carbondale, IL: Southern Illinois University Press, 1969), 183.

36. I am grateful to Dr. Graham McFee for pointing out this distinction concerning intention.

37. Weiss, *Sport: A Philosophic Inquiry*, 183.

38. Saul Ross, "Winning and Losing in Sport: A Radical Reassessment," in *Philosophy of Sport and Physical Activity: Issues and Concepts*, ed. Pasquale J. Galasso (Toronto: Canadian Scholars' Press, 1988), 59.

39. Dunlop, "Bailey on Games, Winning and Education," 154.

40. Peter J. Arnold, "Competitive Sport, Winning and Education," *Journal of Moral Education* 18 (1989): 15-25, 20.

41. David Lyle Light Shields, and Brenda Jo Light Bredemeier, *Character Development and Physical Activity* (Champaign, IL: Human Kinetics, 1995), 218.

42. Jim Parry, "Competitive and Recreative Sport," *British Journal of Physical Education* 9 (1978): 68.

43. Arnold, "Education, Movement, and the Rationality," 66-67.

44. Edwin J. Delattre, "Some Reflections on Success and Failure in Competitive Athletics," in *Philosophic Inquiry in Sport*, ed. William J. Morgan and Klaus V. Meier, 2d ed. (Champaign, IL: Human Kinetics, 1995), 189.

45. See David L. Gallahue, *Understanding Motor Development in Children* (New York: Wiley, 1982); and Robert P. Pangrazi and Victor P. Dauer, *Dynamic Physical Education for Elementary School Children*, 10th ed. (New York: Macmillan Publishing Co., 1992).

46. Lyndon Brown and Steve Grineski, "Competition in Physical Education: An Educational Contradiction?" *Journal of Physical Education, Recreation and Dance* 63 (1992): 17-19, 77.

47. Gallahue, *Understanding Motor Development*; Curt Hinson, "Children and Competition," *Teaching Elementary Physical Education: The Newsletter for Specialists, Teachers, and Administrators* 4 (1993): 17; Jennifer Wall and

Nancy Murray, *Children and Movement: Physical Education in the Elementary School*, 2d ed. (Madison, WI: Brown and Benchmark, 1994).

48. Glyn C. Roberts, "Children in Competition: A Theoretical Perspective and Recommendations for Practice," *Motor Skills: Theory into Practice* 4 (1980): 37-50, 43.

49. Thelma Horn, "On Competition: What the Experts Say," *Teaching Elementary Physical Education: The Newsletter for Specialists, Teachers, and Administrators* 4 (1993): 8-9, 8.

Chapter 5

1. I am grateful to Dr. Murray Elliott for bringing this point to my attention.

2. I must thank one of the anonymous reviewers of *Paideusis* for the "belly button scratching" challenge.

3. Derek C. Meakin, "Moral Values and Physical Education," *Physical Education Review* 5 (1982): 62-82, 65.

4. Ibid.

5. Immanuel Kant, *Foundations of the Metaphysics of Morals*, trans. Lewis White Beck (New York: Bobbs-Merrill, 1959), 39.

6. Aladair MacIntyre, *After Virtue*, 2d ed. (Notre Dame, Indiana: University of Notre Dame Press, 1984), 148.

7. David Carr, "After Kohlberg: Some Implications of an Ethics of Virtue for the Theory of Moral Education and Development," *Studies in Philosophy and Education* 15 (1996): 353-70, 353.

8. Nel Noddings, *Philosophy of Education* (Boulder, CO: Westview Press, 1995), 151-2.

9. Carr, "After Kohlberg," 356.

10. A. Tellings, "A Virtue Approach Instead of a Kantian Approach as a Solution to Major Dilemmas in Meta-Ethics? A Response to David Carr," *Studies in Philosophy and Education* 17 (1998): 47-56, 53.

11. Ibid.

12. Jan W. Steutel, "The Virtue Approach to Moral Education: Some Conceptual Clarifications," *Journal of Philosophy of Education* 31 (1997): 395-407, 400.

13. Ibid.

14. Peter J. Arnold, "Competitive Sport, Winning and Education," *Journal of Moral Education* 18 (1989): 15-25, 23-24.

15. Cornel M. Hamm, *Philosophical Issues in Education: An Introduction* (New York: The Falmer Press, 1989), 141.

16. Derek C. Meakin, "Physical Education: An Agency of Moral Education?" *Journal of the Philosophy of Education* 15 (1981): 241-53, 246.

17. Peter J. Arnold, *Sport, Ethics and Education* (London: Cassell, 1997), 76.

18. Lesley Wright, "Physical Education and Moral Development," *Journal of Philosophy of Education* 21 (1987): 93-102, 96.

19. John R. Searle, *The Construction of Social Reality* (New York: The Free Press, 1995), 27-28.

20. John Rawls, "Two Concepts of Rules," *Philosophical Review* 64 (1955): 3-32, 26-27.

21. See K. O. Apel, "Die ethische Bedeutung des Sports in der Sicht einer Universalistischen Diskursethik," in *Ethische Aspekte des Leistungssports*, ed. E. Franke (Zellerfeld: Clausthal, 1988); and F. de Wachter, "Spielregeln und Ethische Problematik," in *Aktuelle Probleme der Sportphiosophie—Topical Problems of Sportphilosophy*, ed. H. Lenk (Schorndorf: Hofmann, 1983).

22. Johan Steenbergen and Jan Tamboer, "Ethics and the Double Character of Sport: An Attempt to Systematize Discussion of the Ethics of Sport," *Ethics and Sport*, ed. M. J. McNamee and S. J. Parry (London: E and FN Spon, 1998), 39-40.

23. Graham McFee, "Spoiling: An Indirect Reflection of Sport's Moral Imperative?" in *Values in Sport: Elitism, Nationalism, Gender Equality and the Scientific Manufacture of Winners*, ed. Torbjörn Tännsjö and Claudio Tamburrini (London: E and FN Spon, 2000), 172-73.

24. Angela Lumpkin, Sharon Kay Stoll and Jennifer M. Beller, Jennifer M. *Sport Ethics: Applications for Fair Play*, 2d ed. (Boston: WCB/McGraw-Hill, 1999), 6-7.

25. Fred d'Agostino, "The Ethos of Games," *Journal of the Philosophy of Sport* 8 (1981): 7-18, 14.

26. Robert Butcher and Angela Schneider, "Fair Play as Respect for the Game," *Journal of the Philosophy of Sport* 25 (1998): 1-22, 5.

27. David Carr, "What Moral Educational Significance has Physical Education? A Question in Need of Disambiguation," in *Ethics and Sport*, ed. M. J. McNamee and S. J. Parry (London: E and FN Spon, 1998), 129.

28. Wright, "Physical Education and Moral Development," 101.

29. Graham McFee, "Spoiling," 176.

Chapter 6

1. See Bernard F. Booth, "Socio-Cultural Aspects of Play and Moral Development," *Physical Education Review* 4 (1981): 115-20; Grace E. Figley, "Moral Education Through Physical Education," *Quest* 36 (1984): 89-101; T. Romance, "Promoting Character Development in Physical Education," *Strategies* 1 (1988): 16-17; J. F. Brandi, "*A Theory of Moral Development and Competitive School Sport*" (Ph.D. diss., Loyola University of Chicago, 1989); and David Lyle Light Shields and Brenda Jo Light Bredemeier, *Character Development and Physical Activity*. (Champaign, IL: Human Kinetics, 1995).

2. See Peter J. Arnold, "Three Approaches Towards an Understanding of Sportsmanship," *Journal of the Philosophy of Sport* 10 (1984): 61-70; Warren P. Fraleigh, *Right Actions in Sport: Ethics for Contestants* (Champaign, IL: Human Kinetics, 1984); Earle F. Zeigler, *Ethics and Morality in Sport and*

Physical Education: An Experiential Approach (Champaign, IL: Stipes Publishing Company, 1984); Randolph M. Feezell, "Sportsmanship," *Journal of the Philosophy of Sport,* 13 (1986): 1-13; and Edward J. Shea, *Ethical Decisions in Sport: Interscholastic, Intercollegiate, Olympic and Professional,* (Springfield, IL: Charles Thomas, 1996).

3. For example programs, see Thomas J. Martinek and Donald R. Hellison, "Fostering Resiliency in Underserved Youth Through Physical Activity," *Quest* 49 (1997): 33-49; and Stephen C. Miller, Brenda J. L. Bredemeier and David L. L. Shields, Sociomoral Education Through Physical Education with At Risk Children," *Quest* 49 (1997): 114-29.

4. Harvey Siegel, "Critical Thinking as an Educational Ideal," in *Philosophy of Education: Introductory Readings,* ed. William Hare and John Portelli (Calgary, AB: Detselig, 1988), 109.

5. Thomas Donaldson, *Issues in Moral Philosophy* (New York, McGraw-Hill Book Company, 1986), 5-7.

6. Immanuel Kant, *Foundations of the Metaphysics of Morals,* trans. Lewis White Beck (New York: Bobbs-Merrill, 1959), 39.

7. Sheila Wigmore and Cei Tuxill, "A Consideration of the Concept of Fair Play," *European Physical Education Review* 1 (1995): 67-73, 70.

8. Immanuel Kant, *Foundations of the Metaphysics of Morals,* trans. L. Beck (New York: Bobbs-Merrill, 1959), 47.

9. Wigmore and Tuxill, "A Consideration of the Concept of Fair Play," 72.

10. Peter J. Arnold, *Sport, Ethics and Education* (London: Cassell, 1997), 61-62.

11. Donaldson, *Issues in Moral Philosophy,* 6.

12. Paul Davis, "Ethical Issues in Boxing," *Journal of the Philosophy of Sport,* 20/21 (1993/1994): 48-63, 55.

13. Gordon Reddiford, "Morality and the Games Player," *Physical Education Review* 4 (1981): 8-16, 12.

14. Ibid.

15. Davis, "Ethical Issues in Boxing," 51.

16. Richard A. McCormick, "Is Professional Boxing Immoral?" *Sports Illustrated,* 17 (November 5, 1962): 70-82.

17. Arnold, *Sport, Ethics and Education,* 61.

18. Earle F. Zeigler, *Ethics and Morality in Sport and Physical Education: An Experiential Approach* (Champaign, IL: Stipes Publishing Company, 1984), 48-55.

19. Angela Lumpkin, Sharon Kay Stoll and Jennifer M. Beller, Jennifer M. *Sport Ethics: Applications for Fair Play,* 2d ed. (Boston: WCB/McGraw-Hill, 1999), 6.

Chapter 7

1. Joseph Kupfer, "Privacy, Autonomy, and Self-Concept," *American Philosophical Quarterly* 24 (1987): 81-89; Thomas May, "The Concept of Autonomy," *American Philosophical Quarterly* 31 (1994): 133-44; and Michael J. Meyer, "Stoics, Rights, and Autonomy," *American Philosophical Quarterly* 24 (1987): 267-71.
2. Meyer, "Stoics, Rights, and Autonomy," 267.
3. Kupfer, "Privacy, Autonomy, and Self-Concept," 82.
4. May, "The Concept of Autonomy," 134.
5. Aristotle *Politics* 1253a 1-2.
6. Immanuel Kant, *Fundamental Principles of the Metaphysics of Morals*, trans. Thomas K. Abbott (New York: The Liberal Arts Press, 1949), 57.
7. May, "The Concept of Autonomy," 137-38.
8. John Rawls, *A Theory of Justice* (Cambridge: Harvard University Press, 1971), 515.
9. Robert Paul Wolff, *In Defense of Anarchism* (New York: Harper and Row, 1970), 14.
10. Aristotle *Politics* 1276b 20-25, *Politics* 1279a 1-5.
11. May, "The Concept of Autonomy," 141.
12. Aristotle *Nicomachean Ethics* 1104a 5-10.
13. Ibid., 1110a 8-10.
14. May, "The Concept of Autonomy," 141.
15. Ibid.
16. Ibid., 142.
17. Ibid., 141.
18. Kenneth Ravizza and Kathy Daruty, "Paternalism and Sovereignty in Athletics: Limits and Justifications of the Coach's Exercise of Authority Over the Adult Athlete," *Journal of the Philosophy of Sport* 11 (1984): 71-82.
19. Ibid.
20. Ibid., 78-80.
21. Cornel M. Hamm, *Philosophical Issues in Education: An Introduction* (New York: The Falmer Press, 1989), 121.

Chapter 8

1. R. S. Peters, "Education as Initiation," in *Philosophical analysis and education*, ed. Reginald D. Archambault (New York: Humanities Press, 1965), 104.
2. R. S. Peters, *Ethics and Education*. London: George Allen and Unwin, 1966), 32.
3. Ibid.
4. Ibid.
5. Ibid., 34.

6. Martin Lee, "Values and Responsibilities in Children's Sports," *Physical Education Review* 11 (1988): 19-27, 22.

7. See D. Chu, "Functional Myths of Education Organizations: College as Career Training and the Relationship of Formal Title to Actual Duties Upon Secondary School Employees," *NAPHE Proceedings* 11 (1980): 36-46; Linda L. Bain and Janice C. Wendt, "Undergraduate Physical Education Majors' Perceptions of the Roles of Teacher and Coach," *Research Quarterly for Exercise and Sport* 54 (1983): 112-18; Albert J. Figone, "Teacher-Coach Role Conflict: Its Impact on Students and Student-Athletes, *The Physical Educator* 51 (1994): 29-34; Donald F. Staffo, "Clarifying Physical Education Teacher-Coach Responsibilities: A Self-Analysis Guide for Those in Dual Roles," *The Physical Educator* 49 (1992): 52-56; and Thomas J. Templin and Joseph L. Anthrop, "A Dialogue of Teacher/Coach Role Conflict," *The Physical Educator,* 38 (1981): 183-86.

8. Roland G. Tharp and Ronald Gallimore, "What a Coach can Teach a Teacher," *Psychology Today* 9 (1976): 75-78, 76.

9. Staffo, "Clarifying Physical Education Teacher-Coach Responsibilities," 52.

10. Janet Ashburn, "Teacher or Coach," *British Journal of Physical Education* 9 (1978): 36.

11. L. B. Hendry, "Coaches and Teachers of Physical Education: A Comparison of the Personality Dimensions Underlying their Social Orientation," *International Journal of Sport Psychology* 5 (1974): 40-53.

12. Richard W. Field, "Kallinikos: A Dialogue Set in the 20th Century," *Quest* 45 (1993): 357-65, 358.

13. Staffo, "Clarifying Physical Education Teacher-Coach Responsibilities," 53.

14. Lee, "Values and Responsibilities," 21.

15. David Aspin, "Towards a Curriculum for the Education of Coaches: Some Principles and Problems," *Physical Education Review* 6 (1983): 92-100, 98-99.

16. Harvey Siegel, "Critical Thinking as an Educational Ideal," in *Philosophy of Education: Introductory Readings*, ed. William Hare and John Portelli (Calgary, AB: Detselig, 1988).

17. Mike Lane, "Teaching Methods in Coaching," *Coach and Athlete* 4 (1978): 10, 33, 10.

18. Rainer Martens, "Helping Children Become Independent, Responsible Adults Through Sports," in *Competitive Sport for Children and Youth: An Overview of Research and Issues*, ed. Eugene W. Brown and Crystal F. Branta (Champaign, IL: Human Kinetics Books, 1988), 304.

19. Karl Lindholm, "Coaching as Teaching: Seeking Balance," *Phi Delta Kappan* 60 (1979): 734-36, 734.

20. Ibid., 736.

21. See Ken Alexander, Andrew Taggart and Jan Luckman, "Pilgrims Progress: The Sport Education Crusade Down Under," *Journal of Physical*

Education, Recreation and Dance 69 (1988): 21-23; Peter Hastie, "Applied Benefits of the Sport Education Model," *Journal of Physical Education, Recreation and Dance* 69 (1998): 24-26; Daryl Siedentop, "What is Sport Education and How Does it Work?" *Journal of Physical Education, Recreation and Dance* 69 (1998): 18-20.

22. Alexander, Taggart and Luckmann, "Pilgrims Progress," 21.
23. For more details, see Siedentop, "What is Sport Education?"
24. Ibid., 19.
25. Ibid.
26. See Alfie Kohn, *No Contest: The Case Against Competition* (Boston: Houghton Mifflin Company, 1986).
27. Patricia A. Phillips, "The Sport Experience in Education," *Quest* Monograph 23 (1975): 94-97, 97.
28. See Sheila Stanley, *Physical Education: A Movement Orientation.* Toronto: McGraw-Hill, 1969).
29. See Sheryle Bergmann Drewe, *Creative Dance: Enriching Understanding* (Calgary, AB: Detselig Enterprises, 1996).
30. Robert L. Simon, *Fair Play: Sports, Values, and Society.* Boulder, CO: Westview Press, 1991), 23.

Chapter 9

1. See Sheila Stanley, *Physical Education: A Movement Orientation* (Toronto: McGraw-Hill, 1969).
2. See David Best, *Philosophy and Human Movement* (London: George Allen and Unwin, 1978).
3. See Best, *Philosophy and Human Movement*; Drew A. Hyland, *Philosophy of sport* (New York: Paragon House, 1990); Drew Hyland, Drew Hyland, "When Power Becomes Gracious," in *Rethinking College Athletics*, ed. Judith Andre and David N. James (Philadelphia: Temple University Press, 1991); E. F. Kaelin, "The Well-Played Game: Notes Toward an Aesthetics of Sport," *Quest* 10 (1968): 16-28; Joseph Kupfer, "Purpose and Beauty in Sport," *Journal of the Philosophy of Sport* 2 (1975): 83-90; Joseph H. Kupfer, *Experience as Art: Aesthetics in Everyday Life* (Albany, New York: State University of New York Press, 1983); Terence J. Roberts, "Sport, Art, and Particularity: The Best Equivocation," *Journal of the Philosophy of Sport* 13 (1986): 49-63; and Terence J. Roberts, "Sport and Strong Poetry," *Journal of the Philosophy of Sport* 22 (1995): 94-107.
4. J. O. Urmson, "What Makes a Situation Aesthetic?" in *Aristotelian Society Proceedings* suppl. vol. 31 (1957): 75-92, 75-76.
5. Kingsley Price, "What Makes an Experience Aesthetic?" *The British Journal of Aesthetics* 19 (1979): 131-43, 142.

6. Michael H. Mitias, "Can We Speak of 'Aesthetic Experience'?" in *Possibility of the Aesthetic Experience*, ed. Michael H. Mitias (Dordrecht: Martinus Nijohoff Publishers, 1986), 53.

7. Peter Abbs, "The Pattern of Art-Making," in *The Symbolic Order: A Contemporary Reader on the Arts Debate*, ed. Peter Abbs (London: Falmer Press, 1989), 209.

8. Peter Abbs, "Introduction," in *The Symbolic Order: A Contemporary Reader on the Arts Debate*, ed Peter Abbs (London: Falmer Press, 1989), 1.

9. Sheryle Bergmann Drewe, *Creative Dance: Enriching Understanding* (Calgary, AB: Detselig Enterprises, 1996).

10. Peter Abbs, "Aesthetic Education: An Opening Manifesto." in *The symbolic order: A contemporary reader on the arts debate*, ed. Peter Abbs (London: Falmer Press, 1989), 3.

11. E. H. Gombrich, *Art and Illusion: A Study in the Psychology of Pictorial Representation*, 2d ed. (Princeton, NJ: Princeton University Press, 1969), 29.

12. Ibid., 49.

13. Ibid., 195, 202.

14. Rosalind Hursthouse, "Truth and Representation," in *Philosophical Aesthetics: An Introduction*, ed. Oswald Hanfling (Oxford: Blackwell, 1992), 277.

15. Tom Sorell, "Art, Society and Morality," in *Philosophical Aesthetics: An Introduction*, ed. Oswald Hanfling (Oxford: Blackwell, 1992), 307.

16. H. Keller, "Sport and Art–The Concept of Mastery," in *Readings in the Aesthetics of Sport*, ed. H. T. A. Whiting and D. W. Masterson (London: Lepus Books, 1974), 89.

17. Jacques Maquet, *The Aesthetic Experience: An Anthropologist Looks at the Visual Arts* (New Haven: Yale University Press, 1986), 157.

18. Ibid.

19. Best, *Philosophy and Human Movement*, 113.

20. Ibid., 115.

21. Abbs, "Introduction," 1.

22. Richard Shusterman, "Interpretation, Pleasure, and Value in Aesthetic Experience," *The Journal of Aesthetics and Art Criticism* 56 (1998) 51-53, 52.

23. Sharon Bailin, *Achieving Extraordinary Ends: An Essay on Creativity* (Dordrecht: Kluwer Academic Publishers, 1988), 39.

24. Christopher Cordner, "Differences Between Sport and Art," *Journal of the Philosophy of Sport* 15 (1988): 31-47, 37.

25. Best, *Philosophy and Human Movement*, 117.

26. Bergmann Drewe, *Creative Dance*.

27. Cordner, "Differences Between Sport and Art," 38.

28. Hugo A. Meynell, *The Nature of Aesthetic Value* (Albany, New York: State University of New York Press, 1986), 45.

29. Ibid.

30. Ibid.

31. Ibid., 45-46.

32. Geraldine Diamondstein, *Exploring the Arts with Children* (New York: MacMillan Publishing Co., 1974), 30-31.

33. Ibid., 32.

34. Bergmann Drewe, *Creative Dance.*

35. H. Betty Redfern, "Developing and Checking Aesthetic Understanding," in *Aesthetics and Arts Education*, ed. Ralph A. Smith and Alan Simpson (Urbana, Illinois: University of Illinois Press, 1991), 271-72.

36. Stuart Sim, *Beyond Aesthetics: Confrontations with Postructuralism and Postmodernism* (Toronto: University of Toronto Press, 1992), 2.

37. Ibid., 67.

38. Jean-Francois. Lyotard, *The Postmodern Condition: A Report on Knowledge*, trans. Geoff Bennington and Brian Massumi (Manchester: Manchester University Press, 1984), xxiv.

39. Sim, *Beyond Aesthetics*, 87.

40. Ibid., 135.

41. Best, *Philosophy and Human Movement*, 104.

42. Ibid. 43. Ibid., 111-12.

44. Jerrold Levinson, *The Pleasures of Aesthetics: Philosophical Essays* (Ithaca: Cornell University Press, 1996), 231-34.

45. Ibid., 232.

46. Mihaly Csikszentmihalyi, *Beyond Boredom and Anxiety* (San Francisco: Jossey-Bass Publishers, 1975), 36.

47. Kaelin, "The Well-Played Game," 25.

48. Kupfer, "Purpose and Beauty in Sport," 88.

49. Best, *Philosophy and Human Movement*, 104.

50. Ibid.

51. Ibid., 113.

52. Kaelin, "The Well-Played Game," 24.

53. Kupfer, "Purpose and Beauty in Sport," 89.

54. J. M. Boxill, "Beauty, Sport, and Gender," *Journal of the Philosophy of Sport* 11 (1985): 36-47, 45.

Bibliography

Abbs, Peter. "Aesthetic Education: An Opening Manifesto." In *The Symbolic Order: A Contemporary Reader on the Arts Debate*, edited by Peter Abbs. London: Falmer Press, 1989.

Abbs, Peter. "Introduction." In *The Symbolic Order: A Contemporary Reader on the Arts Debate*, edited by Peter Abbs. London: Falmer Press, 1989.

Abbs, Peter. "The Pattern of Art-Making." In *The Symbolic Order: A Contemporary Reader on the Arts Debate*, edited by Peter Abbs. London: Falmer Press, 1989.

Alexander, Ken, Taggart, Andrew, and Jan Luckman. "Pilgrims Progress: The Sport Education Crusade Down Under," *Journal of Physical Education, Recreation and Dance* 69 (1998): 21-23.

Anscombe, G. E. M. *Intention.* Oxford: Basil Blackwell, 1957.

Anscombe, G. E. M. "Modern Moral Philosophy." *Philosophy* 33 (1958): 1-19.

Apel, K. O. "Die ethische Bedeutung des Sports in der Sicht einer Universalistischen Diskursethik." In *Ethische Aspekte des Leistungssports*, edited by E. Franke. Zellerfeld: Clausthal, 1988.

Aristotle. *Nicomachean ethics*

Aristotle. *Politics*

Arnold, Peter J. "Three Approaches Towards an Understanding of Sportsmanship." *Journal of the Philosophy of Sport* 10 (1984): 61-70.

Arnold, Peter J. "Education, Movement, and the Rationality of Practical Knowledge." *Quest* 40 (1988): 115-25.

Arnold, Peter J. "Competitive Sport, Winning and Education." *Journal of Moral Education* 18 (1989): 15-25.

Arnold, Peter J. "The Preeminence of Skill as an Educational Value in the Movement Curriculum." *Quest* 43 (1991): 66-77.

Arnold, Peter J. *Sport, Ethics and Education.* London: Cassell, 1997.

Arnstine, Donald. "The Educator's Impossible Dream: Knowledge as an Educational Aim." In *Philosophy of Education 1992*, edited by H. A. Alexander. Urbana, Illinois: Philosophy of Education Society, 1992.

Ashburn, Janet. "Teacher or Coach." *British Journal of Physical Education* 9 (1978): 36.

Aspin, David. "Towards a Curriculum for the Education of Coaches: Some Principles and Problems." *Physical Education Review* 6 (1983): 92-100.

Bailey, Charles. "Games, Winning and Education." *Cambridge Journal of Education* 5 (1975): 40-50.

Bailin, Sharon. *Achieving Extraordinary Ends: An Essay on Creativity.* Dordrecht: Kluwer Academic Publishers, 1988.

Bain, Linda L., and Janice C. Wendt. "Undergraduate Physical Education Majors' Perceptions of the Roles of Teacher and Coach." *Research Quarterly for Exercise and Sport* 54 (1983): 112-18.

Baron, Robert Steven, Danny Moore, and Glenn S. Sanders. "Distraction as a Source of Drive in Social Facilitation Research." *Journal of Personality and Social Psychology* 36 (1978): 816-24.

Bell, Clive. *Art.* New York: Capricorn Books, 1958.

Bergmann, Sheryle. "An Analysis of the Feminist Critique of the Claims that the Prime Aim of Education is to Develop Critical Thinking." *The Journal of Educational Thought* 28 (1994): 165-78.

Bergmann Drewe, Sheryle. *Creative Dance: Enriching Understanding.* Calgary, AB: Detselig Enterprises, 1996.

Bergmann Drewe, Sheryle. "The Rational Underpinning of Aesthetic Experience: Implications for Arts Education," *Canadian Review of Art* 26 (1999): 22-33.

Best, David. *Philosophy and Human Movement.* London: George Allen and Unwin, 1978.

Booth, Bernard F. "Socio-Cultural Aspects of Play and Moral Development." *Physical Education Review* 4 (1981): 115-20.

Boxill, J. M. "Beauty, Sport, and Gender." *Journal of the Philosophy of Sport* 11 (1985): 36-47.

Brandi, J. *"A Theory of Moral Development and Competitive School Sport."* Ph.D. diss., Loyola University of Chicago, 1989.

Brown, Lyndon, and Steve Grineski, "Competition in Physical Education: An Educational Contradiction?" *Journal of Physical Education, Recreation and Dance* 63 (1992): 17-19, 77.

Burbules, Nicholas. "Reasonable Doubt: Toward a Postmodern Defense of Reason as an Educational Aim." In *Critical Conversations in Philosophy of Education*, edited by Wendy Kohli. New York: Routledge, 1995.

Butcher, Robert, and Angela Schneider. "Fair Play as Respect for the Game." *Journal of the Philosophy of Sport,* 25 (1998): 1-22.

Campbell, David N. "On Being Number One: Competition in Education." *Phi Delta Kappan* 56 (1974): 143-46.

Carr, David. "Practical Reasoning and Knowing How." *Journal of Human Movement Studies* 4 (1978): 3-20.

Carr, David. "Aims of Physical Education." *Physical Education Review* 2 (1979): 91-100.

Carr, David. "Knowledge in Practice." *American Philosophical Quarterly* 18 (1981): 53-61.

Carr, David. "After Kohlberg: Some Implications of an Ethics of Virtue for the Theory of Moral Education and Development." *Studies in Philosophy and Education* 15 (1996): 353-70.

Carr, David. "What Moral Educational Significance has Physical Education? A Question in Need of Disambiguation." In *Ethics and Sport*, edited by M. J. McNamee and S. J. Parry. London: E and FN Spon, 1998.

Chu, D. "Functional Myths of Education Organizations: College as Career Training and the Relationship of Formal Title to Actual Duties upon Secondary School Employees." *NAPHE Proceedings* 11 (1980): 36-46.

Cleland, Fran, and Cynthia Pearse. "Critical Thinking in Elementary Physical Education. Reflections on a Year Long Study." *Journal of Physical Education, Recreation and Dance* 66 (1995): 31-38.

Coakley, Jay J. *Sport in Society: Issues and Controversies.* 5th ed. St. Louis, MO: Mosby, 1994.

Colbeck, John. "Against Reason." *Revista espanola de pedagogia* ano L (1992): 515-25.

Cordner, Christopher. "Differences Between Sport and Art." *Journal of the Philosophy of Sport* 15 (1988): 31-47.

Crawford, Donald W. "The Questions of Aesthetics." In *Aesthetics and Arts Education*, edited by Ralph A. Smith and Alan Simpson. Illinois: University of Illinois Press, 1991.

Csikszentmihalyi, Mihaly. *"Beyond Boredom and Anxiety."* San Francisco: Jossey-Bass Publishers, 1975.

d'Agostino, Fred. "The Ethos of Games." *Journal of the Philosophy of Sport* 8 (1981): 7-18.

Dakin, Stephen, and A. John Arrowood, "The Social Comparison of Ability." *Human Relations* 34 (1981): 89-109.

Davis, Paul. "Ethical Issues in Boxing." *Journal of the Philosophy of Sport* 20/21 (1993/1994): 48-63.

Delattre, Edwin J. "Some Reflections on Success and Failure in Competitive Athletics." In *Philosophic Inquiry in Sport*, edited by William J. Morgan and Klaus V. Meier. 2d ed. Champaign, IL: Human Kinetics, 1995.

Derrida, Jacques. *Signéponge=Signsponge.* Translated by Richard Rand. New York: Columbia University Press, 1984.

Diamondstein, Geraldine. *Exploring the Arts with Children.* New York: MacMillan Publishing Co., 1974.

Donaldson, Thomas. *Issues in Moral Philosophy.* New York, McGraw-Hill Book Company, 1986.

Downie, R. S., Eileen M. Loudfoot, and Elizabeth Telfer, E. *Education and Personal Relationships.* London: Methuen and Co., 1974.

Dunlop, Francis "Bailey on Games, Winning and Education." *Cambridge Journal of Education* 5 (1975): 153-60.

Dworkin, Ronald. *Taking Rights Seriously.* Cambridge, MA: Harvard University Press, 1977.

Ennis, Robert H. "A Concept of Critical Thinking." *Harvard Educational Review* 32 (1962) 81-111.

Ennis, Robert H. "A Taxonomy of Critical Thinking Dispositions and Abilities." In *Teaching Thinking Skills: Theory and Practice*, edited by Joan Boykoff Baron and Robert J. Sternberg. New York: W. H. Freeman, 1987.

Ennis, Robert H. "The Degree to Which Critical Thinking is Subject Specific: Clarification and Needed Research." In *The Generalizability of Critical Thinking: Multiple Perspectives on an Educational Ideal*, edited by Stephen P. Norris. New York: Teachers College Press, 1992.

Fait, Hollis F., and John E. Billing. "Reassessment of the Value of Competition." In *Joy and Sadness in Children's Sports*, edited by Rainer Martens. Champaign, IL: Human Kinetics, 1978.

Feezell, Randolph M. "Sportsmanship." *Journal of the Philosophy of Sport* 13 (1986): 1-13.

Feinberg, Joel. *Harm to Self*. Oxford: Oxford University Press, 1986.

Festinger, Leon. "A Theory of Social Comparison Processes." *Human Relations* 7 (1954): 117-40.

Field, Richard, W. "Kallinikos: A Dialogue Set in the 20th Century." *Quest* 45 (1993): 357-65.

Fielding, M. "Against Competition." *Proceedings of the Philosophy of Education Society of Great Britain* 10 (1976): 124-46.

Figley, Grace E. "Moral Education through Physical Education." *Quest* 36 (1984): 89-101.

Figone, Albert J. "Teacher-Coach Role Conflict: Its Impact on Students and Student Athletes." *The Physical Educator* 51 (1994): 29-34.

Fraleigh, Warren P. *Right Actions in Sport: Ethics for Contestants*. Champaign, IL: Human Kinetics, 1984.

Gallahue, David L. *Understanding Motor Development in Children*. New York: Wiley, 1982.

Gastorf, John, Jerry Suls, and John Lawhon. "Opponent Choices of Below Average Performers." *Bulletin of the Psychonomic Society* 12 (1978): 217-20.

Gombrich, E. H. *Art and Illusion: A Study in the Psychology of Pictorial Representation*. 2d ed. Princeton, NJ: Princeton University Press, 1969.

Grineski, Steve. "Children, Cooperative Learning, and Physical Education." *Teaching Elementary Physical Education* 4 (1993): 10-14.

Greenockle, Karen M., and Gracie J. Purvis. "Redesigning a Secondary School Wellness Unit Using the Critical Thinking Model." *Journal of Physical Education, Recreation, and Dance* 66 (1995): 49-52.

Groff, Bradford D., Robert S. Baron, and D. L. Moore, D. L. "Distraction, Attentional Conflict, and Drive-Like Behavior." *Journal of Experimental Social Psychology* 19 (1983): 359-80.

Hamm, Cornel M. *Philosophical Issues in Education: An Introduction*. New York: The Falmer Press, 1989.

Hampshire, Stuart *Thought and Action*. London: Chatto and Windus, 1959.

Hastie, Peter. "Applied Benefits of the Sport Education Model." *Journal of Physical Education, Recreation and Dance* 69 (1998): 24-26.

Hautala, Robert M. "Enhancing Games Through Critical Thinking." *Teaching Elementary Physical Education* 2 (1991): 8-9.

Hendry, L. "Coaches and Teachers of Physical Education: A Comparison of the Personality Dimensions Underlying Their Social Orientation." *International Journal of Sport Psychology* 5 (1974): 40-53.

Hinson, Curt. "Children and Competition." *Teaching Elementary Physical Education The Newsletter for Specialists, Teachers, and Administrators* 4 (1993): 17.

Hirst, P. H., and R. S. Peters. *The Logic of Education*. London: Routledge and Kegan Paul, 1970.

Hirst, Paul H. "Liberal Education and the Nature of Knowledge." In *The Philosophy of Education*, edited by R. S. Peters. Oxford: Oxford University Press, 1973.

Hirst, Paul H. *Knowledge and the Curriculum*. London: Routledge and Kegan Paul, 1974.

Hirst, Paul H. "Education, Knowledge and Practices." In *Beyond Liberal Education Essays in Honour of Paul H. Hirst*, edited by Robin Barrow and Patricia White. London: Routledge, 1993.

Horn, Thelma. "On Competition: What the Experts Say." *Teaching Elementary Physical Education: The Newsletter for Specialists, Teachers, and Administrators* 4 (1993): 8-9.

Hospers, John. *Understanding the Arts*. Englewood Cliffs, NJ: Prentice-Hall, 1982.

Hursthouse, Rosalind. "Truth and Representation." In *Philosophical Aesthetics: An Introduction*, edited by Oswald Hanfling. Oxford: Blackwell, 1992.

Hyland, Drew A. "Competition and Friendship." In *Philosophic Inquiry in Sport*, edited by William J. Morgan and Klaus V. Meier. 1st ed. Champaign, IL: Human Kinetics, 1988.

Hyland, Drew A. *Philosophy of Sport*. New York: Paragon House, 1990.

Hyland, Drew. "When Power Becomes Gracious." In *Rethinking College Athletics*, edited by Judith Andre and David N. James. Philadelphia: Temple University Press, 1991.

Johnson, Ralph H. "The Problem of Defining Critical Thinking." In *The Generalizability of Critical Thinking: Multiple Perspectives on an Educational Ideal*, edited by Stephen P. Norris New York: Teachers College Press, 1992.

Kaelin, E. F. "The Well-Played Game: Notes Toward an Aesthetics of Sport." *Quest* 10 (1968): 16-28.

Kant, Immanuel. *Foundations of the Metaphysics of Morals*. Translated by Lewis White Beck. New York: Bobbs-Merrill, 1959.

Kant, Immanuel. *Fundamental Principles of the Metaphysics of Morals*. Translated by Thomas K. Abbott. New York: The Liberal Arts Press, 1949.

Keating, James W. "The Ethics of Competition and its Relation to Some Moral Problems in Athletics." In *The Philosophy of Sport: A Collection of Original Essays*, edited by Robert G. Osterhoudt. Springfield, IL: Thomas, 1973.

Keller, H. "Sport and Art–The Concept of Mastery." In *Readings in the Aesthetics of Sport*, edited by H. T. A. Whiting and D. W. Masterson. London: Lepus Books, 1974.

Kenny, Anthony. "Practical Inference." *Analysis* 26 (1966): 65-75.

Kildea, Alice E. "Competition: A Model for Conception." *Quest*, 35 (1983): 169-81.

Kirchner, Glenn. *Physical Education for Elementary School Children*, 8th ed. Dubuque, IA: Wm. C. Brown Publishers, 1992.

Kohn, Alfie. *No Contest: The Case Against Competition*. Boston: Houghton Mifflin Company, 1986.

Kretchmar, Scott. "Ontological Possibilities: Sport as Play." In *Philosophic Exchange The Annual Proceedings of the Center for Philosophic Exchange*, 1972.

Kretchmar, R. Scott. *Practical Philosophy of Sport*. Champaign, Illinois: Human Kinetics, 1994.

Kupfer, Joseph. "Purpose and Beauty in Sport." *Journal of the Philosophy of Sport* 2 (1975): 83-90.

Kupfer, Joseph H. *Experience as Art: Aesthetics in Everyday Life*. Albany, New York: State University of New York Press, 1983.

Kupfer, Joseph. "Privacy, Autonomy, and Self-Concept." *American Philosophical Quarterly* 24 (1987): 81-89.

Lane, Mike. "Teaching Methods in Coaching." *Coach and Athlete* 4 (1978) 10, 33.

Lee, Martin. "Values and Responsibilities in Children's Sports." *Physical Education Review* 11 (1988): 19-27.

Levinson, Jerrold. *The Pleasures of Aesthetics: Philosophical Essays*. Ithaca: Cornell University Press, 1996.

Lindholm, Karl. "Coaching as Teaching: Seeking Balance." *Phi Delta Kappan* 60 (1979): 734-36.

Lipman, Matthew. *Thinking in Education*. Cambridge: Cambridge University Press, 1991.

Lipman, Matthew. "Good Thinking." *Inquiry: Critical Thinking Across the Disciplines* 15 (1995): 37-41.

Lumpkin, Angela, Sharon Kay Stoll, and Jennifer M. Beller. *Sport Ethics Applications for Fair Play*. 2d ed. St. Louis: Mosby, 1994.

Lyotard, Jean-Francois. *The Postmodern Condition: A Report on Knowledge*. Translated by Geoff Bennington and Brian Massumi. Manchester: Manchester University Press, 1984.

MacIntyre, Alasdair C. "Against Utilitarianism." In *Aims in Education: The Philosophic Approach*, edited by T. H. B. Hollins. Manchester: Manchester University Press, 1964.

MacIntyre, Alasdair. *After Virtue*, 2d ed. Notre Dame, Indiana: University of Notre Dame Press, 1984.

Macmillan, C. J. B. "Love and Logic in 1984." In *Philosophy of Education 1984*, edited by Emily E. Robertson. Illinois State University: Philosophy of Education Society, 1984.

Maquet, Jacques. *The Aesthetic Experience: An Anthropologist Looks at the Visual Arts*. New Haven: Yale University Press, 1986.

Martens, Fred L. *Basic Concepts of Physical Education: The Foundations in Canada*. Champaign, Illinois: Stipes Publishing Company, 1986.

Martens, Rainer. "Helping Children Become Independent, Responsible Adults Through Sports." In *Competitive Sport for Children and Youth: An Overview of Research and Issues*, edited by Eugene W. Brown and Crystal F. Branta. Champaign, IL: Human Kinetics Books, 1988.

Martinek, Thomas J., and Hellison, Donald R. "Fostering Resiliency in Underserved Youth Through Physical Activity." *Quest* 49 (1997): 33-49.

May, Thomas. "The Concept of Autonomy." *American Philosophical Quarterly*, 31 (1994): 133-44.

McBride, Ron E. "Critical Thinking–An Overview with Implications for Physical Education." *Journal of Teaching in Physical Education* 11 (1991): 112-25.

McCormick, Richard A. "Is Professional Boxing Immoral?" *Sports Illustrated* 17 (November 5, 1962): 70-82.

McFee, Graham. "Spoiling: An Indirect Reflection of Sport's Moral Imperative?" In *Values in Sport: Elitism, Nationalism, Gender Equality and the Scientific Manufacture of Winners*, edited by Torbjörn Tännsjö and Claudio Tamburrini. London: E and FN Spon, 2000.

McIntosh, Peter. *Fair Play: Ethics in Sport and Education*. London: Heinemann, 1979.

McPeck, John E. *Critical Thinking and Education*. New York: St. Martin's Press, 1981.

Meakin, Derek C. "Physical Education: An Agency of Moral Education?" *Journal of the Philosophy of Education* 15 (1981): 241-53.

Meakin, Derek C. "Moral Values and Physical Education." *Physical Education Review* 5 (1982): 62-82.

Meakin, Derek C. "How Physical Education can Contribute to Personal and Social Education." *Physical Education Review* 2 (1990): 108-19.

Metheny, Eleanor. *Vital Issues*. Washington, DC: American Alliance for Health, Physical Education, and Recreation, 1977.

Meyer, Michael. "Stoics, Rights, and Autonomy." *American Philosophical Quarterly* 24 (1987): 267-71.

Meynell, Hugo A. *The Nature of Aesthetic Value*. Albany, New York: State University of New York Press, 1986.

Miller, Stephen, Brenda J. L. Bredemeier, and David L. L. Shields. "Sociomoral Education Through Physical Education with At Risk Children." *Quest* 49 (1997): 114-29.

Mitias, Michael H. "Can We Speak of 'Aesthetic Experience'?" In *Possibility of the Aesthetic Experience*, edited by Michael H. Mitias. Dordrecht: Martinus Nijohoff Publishers, 1986.

Munrow, A. D. *Physical Education: A Discussion of Principles.* London: G. Bell and Sons, 1972.

Nichols, Beverly. *Moving and Learning: The Elementary School Physical Education Experience.* 3d ed. St. Louis: Mosby, 1994.

Noddings, Nel. *Philosophy of Education.* Boulder, CO: Westview Press, 1995.

Orlick, Terry. *Winning Through Cooperation: Competitive Insanity, Cooperative Alternatives.* Washington, DC: Acropolis Books, 1978.

Pangrazi, Robert P, and Victor P. Dauer. *Dynamic Physical Education for Elementary School Children.* 10th ed. New York: Macmillan Publishing Co., 1992.

Parry, Jim. "Competitive and Recreative Sport." *British Journal of Physical Education* 9 (1978): 68.

Parry, Jim. "Physical Education, Justification and the National Curriculum." *Physical Education Review* 11 (1988): 106-18.

Paul, Richard. "Teaching Critical Thinking in the 'Strong' Sense: A Focus on Self-Deception, World Views, and a Dialectical Mode of Analysis." *Informal Logic Newsletter* 4 (1982): 2-7.

Paul, Richard. *Critical Thinking: What Every Person Needs to Survive in a Rapidly Changing World.* 3rd ed., rev. Santa Rosa, CA: Foundation for Critical Thinking, 1993.

Paul, Richard. "Understanding Substantive Critical Thinking: Avoiding the Growing List of Counterfeits." *Critical Thinking: Events and Resources for College and University Educators.* Santa Rosa, CA: The Center and Foundation for Critical Thinking (Spring 1995): 7-11.

Perry, L. "Competition and Cooperation." *British Journal of Educational Studies* 23 (1975): 127-34.

Peters, R. S. "Education as Initiation." In *Philosophical Analysis and Education*, edited by Reginald D. Archambault. New York: Humanities Press, 1965.

Peters, R. S. *Ethics and Education.* London: George Allen and Unwin, 1966.

Peters, R. S. "What is an educational process?" In *The Concept of Education*, edited by R. S. Peters. London: Routledge and Kegan Paul, 1967.

Phillips, Patricia A. "The Sport Experience in Education." *Quest* Monograph 23 (1975): 94-97.

Price, Kingsley. "What Makes an Experience Aesthetic?" *The British Journal of Aesthetics* 19 (1979): 131-43.

Ravizza, Kenneth, and Daruty, Kathy. "Paternalism and Sovereignty in Athletics: Limits and Justifications of the Coach's Exercise of Authority Over the Adult Athlete." *Journal of the Philosophy of Sport* 11 (1984): 71-82.

Rawls, John. "Two Concepts of Rules." *Philosophical Review* 64 (1955): 3-32.

Rawls, John. *A Theory of Justice.* Cambridge: Harvard University Press, 1971.

Reddiford, Gordon. "Morality and the Games Player." *Physical Education Review* 4 (1981): 8-16.

Redfern, H. Betty. "Developing and Checking Aesthetic Understanding." In *Aesthetics and Arts Education*, Ralph A. Smith and Alan Simpson. Urbana, Illinois: University of Illinois Press, 1991.

Reid, Andrew. "Value Pluralism and Physical Education." *European Physical Education Review* 3 (1997): 6-20.

Richmond, Stuart. "Once Again: Art Education, Politics, and the Aesthetic Perspective." *Canadian Review of Art Education* 16 (1989): 119-128.

Roberts, Glyn C. "Children in Competition: A Theoretical Perspective and Recommendations for Practice." *Motor Skills: Theory into Practice* 4 (1980): 37-50.

Roberts, Terence J. "Sport, Art, and Particularity: The Best Equivocation." *Journal of the Philosophy of Sport* 13 (1986): 49-63.

Roberts, Terence J. "Sport and Strong Poetry." *Journal of the Philosophy of Sport* 22 (1995) 94-107.

Romance, T. "Promoting Character Development in Physical Education." *Strategies* 1 (1988): 16-17.

Rorty, Richard. "Solidarity or Objectivity?" In *Relativism: Interpretation and Confrontation*, edited by Michael Krauz. Notre Dame: University of Notre Dame Press, 1989). Quoted in Harvey Siegel, "On Some Recent Challenges to the Ideal of Reason." *Inquiry: Critical Thinking Across the Disciplines* 15 (1996): 2-16.

Ross, Saul. *Persons, Minds and Bodies: A Transcultural Dialogue Amongst Physical Education, Philosophy and the Social Sciences.* North York, Ontario: University of Toronto Press, 1988.

Ross, Saul. "Winning and Losing in Sport: A Radical Reassessment." In *Philosophy of Sport and Physical Activity: Issues and Concepts*, edited by Pasquale J. Galasso. Toronto: Canadian Scholars' Press, 1988.

Ryle, Gilbert. *The Concept of Mind.* London: Hutchinson, 1949.

Schaar, John H. "Equality of Opportunity and Beyond." In *Equality, Nomos* 9, edited by J. Roland Pennock and John W. Chapman. New York: Atherton Press, 1967.

Schacht, Richard. "On Weiss on Records, Athletic Activity, and the Athlete." In *Philosophic Exchange: The Annual Proceedings of the Center for Philosophic Exchange*, 1972.

Schwager, Susan, and Cathy Labate. "Teaching for Critical Thinking in Physical Education." *Journal of Physical Education, Recreation and Dance* 64 (1993): 24-26.

Searle, John R. *The Construction of Social Reality.* New York: The Free Press, 1995.

Shea, Edward J. *Ethical Decisions in Sport: Interscholastic, Intercollegiate, Olympic and Professional.* Springfield, IL: Charles Thomas, 1996.

Shields, David Lyle Light, and Brenda Jo Light Bredemeier. *Character Development and Physical Activity.* Champaign, IL: Human Kinetics, 1995.

Shusterman, Richard. "Interpretation, Pleasure, and Value in Aesthetic Experience." *The Journal of Aesthetics and Art Criticism* 56 (1998): 51-53.

Siedentop, Daryl. "What is Sport Education and How Does it Work?" *Journal of Physical Education, Recreation and Dance* 69 (1998): 18-20.

Siegel, Harvey. "Critical Thinking as an Educational Ideal." In *Philosophy of Education: Introductory Readings*, edited by W. Hare and J. Portelli. Calgary, AB:. Detselig, 1988.

Siegel, Harvey. *Educating Reason: Rationality, Critical Thinking, and Education.* New York: Routledge, 1988.

Siegel, Harvey. "The Generalizability of Critical Thinking Skills, Dispositions, and Epistemology." In *The Generalizability of Critical Thinking: Multiple Perspectives on an Educational Ideal*, edited by Stephen P. Norris. New York: Teachers College Press, 1992.

Siegel, Harvey. "On Some Recent Challenges to the Ideal of Reason." *Inquiry: Critical Thinking Across the Disciplines* 15 (1996): 2-16.

Siegel, Harvey. *Rationality Redeemed? Further Dialogues on an Educational Ideal.* New York: Routledge, 1997.

Sim, Stuart. *Beyond Aesthetics: Confrontations with Postructuralism and Postmodernism.* Toronto: University of Toronto Press, 1992.

Simon, Robert L. *Fair Play: Sports, Values, and Society.* Boulder, CO: Westview Press, 1991.

Smoll, Frank L., and Ronald E. Smith, eds. *Children and Youth in Sport: A Biopsychosocial Perspective.* Madison, WI: Brown and Benchmark, 1996.

Sorell, Tom. "Art, Society and Morality." In *Philosophical Aesthetics: An Introduction*, edited by Oswald Hanfling. Oxford: Blackwell, 1992.

Staffo, Donald F. "Clarifying Physical Education Teacher-Coach Responsibilities: A Self-Analysis Guide for Those in Dual Roles." *The Physical Educator* 49 (1992): 52-56.

Stanley, Sheila. *Physical Education: A Movement Orientation.* Toronto: McGraw-Hill, 1969.

Steenbergen, Johan, and Jan Tamboer. "Ethics and the Double Character of Sport: An Attempt to Systematize Discussion of the Ethics of Sport." In *Ethics and Sport*, edited by M. J. McNamee and S. J. Parry. London: E and FN Spon, 1998.

Steutel, Jan W. "The Virtue Approach to Moral Education: Some Conceptual Clarifications." *Journal of Philosophy of Education* 31 (1997): 395-407.

Suls, Jerry M., and R. L. Miller, eds. *Social Comparison Processes: Theoretical and Empirical Perspectives.* Washington, DC: Hemisphere, 1977.

Tellings, A. "A Virtue Approach Instead of a Kantian Approach as a Solution to Major Dilemmas in Meta-Ethics? A Response to David Carr." *Studies in Philosophy and Education* 17 (1998): 47-56.

Templin, Thomas J., and Joseph L. Anthrop. "A Dialogue of Teacher/Coach Role Conflict." *The Physical Educator* 38 (1981): 183-86.

Tharp, Roland G., and Ronald Gallimore, "What a Coach can Teach a Teacher." *Psychology Today* 9 (1976): 75-78.

Thayer-Bacon, Barbara J. "Caring and its Relationship to Critical Thinking." *Educational Theory* 43 (1993): 323-40.

Thomas, Carolyn. *Sport in a Philosophic Context*. Philadelphia: Lea and Febiger, 1983.

Tishman, Shari, and David N. Perkins, "Critical Thinking and Physical Education." *Journal of Physical Education, Recreation, and Dance* 66 (1995): 24-30.

Tutko, Thomas, and William Bruns. *Winning is Everything and Other American Myths*. New York: Macmillan, 1976.

Urmson, J. O. "What Makes a Situation Aesthetic?" In *Aristotelian Society Proceedings* suppl. vol. 31 (1957): 75-92.

Vanderswaag, Harold J. *Toward a Philosophy of Sport*. Reading, Massachusetts: Addison-Wesley Publishing Company, 1972.

Wachter, F. de. "Spielregeln und Ethische Problematik." In *Aktuelle Probleme der Sportphiosophie—Topical Problems of Sportphilosophy*, edited by H. Lenk. Schorndorf: Hofmann, 1983.

Wall, Jennifer, and Nancy Murray. *Children and Movement: Physical Education in the Elementary School*. 2d ed. Madison, WI: Brown and Benchmark, 1994.

Weiss, Paul. *Sport: A Philosophic Inquiry*. Carbondale, IL: Southern Illinois University Press, 1969.

White, John. *The Aims of Education Restated*. London: Routledge and Kegan Paul, 1982.

Wigmore, Sheila, and Cei Tuxill. "A Consideration of the Concept of Fair Play." *European Physical Education Review* 1 (1995): 67-73.

Williams, Kevin. "On Learning for its Own Sake." *Prospero* 3 (1997): 10-13.

Wittgenstein, Ludwig. *Philosophical Investigations*. Translated by G.E.M. Anscombe. New York: Macmillan, 1953.

Wolff, Robert Paul. *In Defense of Anarchism*. New York: Harper and Row, 1970.

Wright, Lesley. "Physical Education and Moral Development." *Journal of Philosophy of Education* 21 (1987): 93-102.

Zajonc, Robert B. "Attitudinal Effects of Mere Exposure." *Journal of Personality and Social Psychology* Monograph Supplement 9 (1968): 1-27.

Zeigler, Earle R., and K. J. McCristal. "A History of the Big Ten Body-of-Knowledge Project in Physical Education." *Quest* 9 (1967): 79-84.

Zeigler, Earle R. *Ethics and Morality in Sport and Physical Education: An Experiential Approach*. Champaign, IL: Stipes Publishing Company, 1984.

INDEX